To Dance in the Downpour of Devotion

by Vraja Kishor das

Proofing by Kadamba Māla dāsī

First Edition: July 24, 2013

ISBN: 1491090278
ISBN-13: 978-1491090275

Contents

Introduction

This book is for people like you and me, who want to transform ourselves from the abject ignorance of self-absorption to the ever-escalating bliss of divine love. It is a retelling, almost an outright translation, of a renaissance Sanskrit book entitled *The Downpour of Sweetness*,[1] which is itself an illumination upon three famous lines of an earlier treatise, *The Ambrosial Ocean of Devotion*:[2]

> *The path to divine love has nine stages. (1) First comes conviction, then (2) guidance, (3) practice, (4) purification, and (5) fixedness. Next arises (6) taste, which then becomes (7) addiction. At long last there is (8) awakening and finally attainment of the ultimate goal: (9) divine love.*[3]

---

[1] *Mādhurya Kadambinī* by Viśvanātha Chakravartī Ṭhākur
[2] *Bhakti Rasāmṛta Sindhu* by Rūpa Goswāmī
[3] BRS 1.4.15-16: *ādau śraddhā tataḥ sādhu-saṅgo 'tha bhajana-kriyā | tato 'nartha-nivṛttiḥ syāt tato niṣṭhā rucis tataḥ | athāsaktis tato bhāvas tataḥ premābhyudaṣcati*

To Dance in the Downpour of Devotion is a guide through very practical and fascinating nuances and details of these nine stages. Think of it as a road map for your journey from ignorance to bliss.

May Śrī Śrī Vṛṣabhanu-Nandini Nanda-nandana, radiating the unlimited kindness of Śrī Śrī Gadai Gaura, bless the author and each reader with swift, sure, and deep realization of its every line.

Invocation

In the midst of summer's stifling heat,
From out of the blue,
A monsoon cloud approaches,
Hovering majestically low.

The cloud is Śrī Krishna Caitanya Mahāprabhu: the divine beloved (Śrī Krishna), taking the personality and perspective of the divine lover (Śrī Rādhā). He is the Supreme Personality of Divine Love.

Mahāprabhu is like a cloud because he carries the rainwater of ecstatic divine love from the ocean of Śrīmatī Rādhārāṇī's infinite compassion, and showers it upon the thirsty hearts of we who are pathetically divorced, separated, and cut-off from the spiritual world, eternally wallowing in a drought of true love, happiness, and significance.

Clouds appear from out of the blue, just as Mahāprabhu's compassionate downpour of spiritual love is an act of spontaneous, unscripted, unforeseeable, self-authorizing, sweet, and opulent freewill.

The burning summer heat of materialism is scorched by the blaring rays of the "Sun" - the blazingly arrogant, autocratic, and ruthless ego. Mahāprabhu's compassion is a monsoon cloud appearing at the apex of this summer, instantly shattering its oppressive heat before the first drop of rain even falls!

Parched fields rejoice
  in its cooling shade,
Soak
  in its blissful downpour,
Blossom
  with abundant crops:
A rich harvest
  of nine-fold devotions.

The downpour falls upon parched fields, which symbolize the human heart. It soaks these fields, makes them fertile, and allows nine crops to grow: the nine expressions of divine love, which quickly yield their abundantly blissful harvest.[1]

Far off, behind mountain walls
in a barren desert,
The ruined shell of a decimated tree
stands forlorn,
But, catching a faint scent of mist
from that distant downpour,
She rejoices, feels renewed,
and blossoms!

Not every heart is as receptive as a tilled field. Some hearts, like mine, hide behind mountain-walls of solid rock, sheer cliffs of ego-centrism. All that can grow there, in that desert devoid of spiritual mercy, is a mangled, twisted, and decimated tree. But, the downpour of mercy in Mahāprabhu's monsoon is so sweet and profuse

[1] These nine are (1) Hearing about, (2) talking about, (3) remembering, (4) assisting, (5) worshipping, (6) beseeching, (7) serving, (8) befriending, and (9) becoming soul-mates with the divine beloved. (See *Bhāgavata Purāṇa* 7.5.23)

that even a slight mist of it born on the distant winds is enough to revive and refresh the briar-ridden thorn-land of my barren heart!

The downpour runs off rocky hillsides,
to form a flooding river
Rising
to rush life-giving moisture
to the far corners of the world.

Renewing the ancient riverbed of divine love
In which great souls throughout history
have bathed.

Mahāprabhu's mercy is not limited to those fortunate persons who were near him in time and space. His mercy forms a river that flows through time and space to irrigate the far corners of the world.

It flows in an ancient riverbed, dug by primordial sages like Nārada Muni to carry divine mercy through the vast expanse of history.

A lovely boat appears on the river
Guided by the expert hand of Śrī Rūpa,
The most intimate
of divine lovers
of Śrī Krishna.

Navigating this river is a lovely boat, driven by the most expert divine lover of Krishna, Śrī Rūpa. When people from all over the world board this boat, Śrī Rūpa guides them along the river of Mahāprabhu's mercy and into the ambrosial ocean of devotion.

In this boat
Śrī Rūpa will take us
To the most confidential,
sublime depths
Of the ocean of intimate divine love.

Śrī Rūpa is the foremost guru of divine love. Other great souls assist Śrī Rūpa to expand the river and build new ports.

The river did not fully cross the Himalayan border until the most compassionate of all Śrī Rūpa's followers, A.C. Bhaktivedānta Swāmī Prabhupāda, fearlessly extended its riverbed into every town and village across the globe.

Half-knowingly, I boarded at a port opened boldly into the mosh pits of the youth of today by Prabhupāda's assistant Śrīpāda Dhanurdhara Swāmī, and his own assistant Śrīman Raghunātha Dāsa. And so it is, against infinite odds, that today I find myself pushed by the flow of this river of divine mercy to write a book entitled *To Dance in the Downpour of Delight*. May it augment the current of that beautiful river, drenching our hearts in eternally fascinating intoxication with the divine couple, Śrī Śrī Rādhā-Krishna.

Chapter One

What is Divine Love?

What is "love"?

Love is a tangible expression of the motivation to please someone.[1]

What is "*true* love"?

Love is *true* and *pure* when it is free from all self-interest, and thus expressed even at one's own expense.[2]

What is "*divine* love"?

True love is divine when the beloved is divine.

---

[1] *Bhakti Rasāmṛta Sindhu* 1.1.11: *ānukūlyena, anuśīlanam*
[2] *Bhakti Rasāmṛta Sindhu* 1.1.11: *anyābhilāṣitā śūnyam*

So, pure divine love is a tangible expression of the intention to please Krishna, undiluted by other endeavors and untainted by ulterior motives.

Who is the Divine Beloved?

The *Upanishads* beautifully define The Divine:

> *The Divine - beyond even the very substance of existence - is the ultimate source of all fascinating ecstatic emotions. Obtain him and be blissful.*[1]

According to this, The Divine is the original fountainhead of all *emotion*. Emotion is a subjective reality experienced by conscious beings: persons. Thus if The Divine is the origin of emotion, The Divine must be a *personal* being.

But before revealing him as a person, the *Upanishads* first go to great lengths to establish The Divine as "an entity beyond even the substance of existence." By doing so, they help us comprehend that The Divine no ordinary person. Being the *supreme* person - The Divine is beyond any flaws or limitations, and thus able to

---

[1] *Taittiriya Upanishad* (*Ananda Valli*.7): [...] *raso vai saḥ. rasaṁ hy evāyaṁ labdhvānandi bhavati.*

reciprocate divine love flawlessly and limitlessly. Thus, "He is bliss. Love him and be blissful."

The *Upanishads* inform us that the Divine Beloved is a person beyond the limits of reality who infinitely delights us by perfectly reciprocating and amplifying all our love. The Sanskrit encapsulates all of this meaning is, "Krishna."

Thus it is understood that the divine beloved is Krishna.

On one hand, this statement is a linguistic and conceptual truism. On the other, it is controversial because there is a historical personality named Krishna. Do we mean to say that *this* Krishna, the son of Vasudeva, is the Divine Beloved?

Yes - but *inclusively*.

The *Upanishads* defined The Divine as "beyond the very substance of existence itself." Does Krishna meet this criterion? Sanskrit spiritual literature consistently defines Krishna in such a manner, and he himself admits it in *Bhagavad Gītā*:

I am beyond the limitations of existence because I am the foundation of the very substance of existence.[1]

Is Krishna the *only* being beyond the limitations of existence? No. There are infinite forms of Godhead - all of them are valid objects of divine love. But among them all Krishna is unique, because no other form of Godhead reciprocates love as fully and unabashedly as he.

Most forms of divinity are prominently powerful, majestic, and even awful. With them, divine love is possible only in a formal, orderly fashion expressed through loyal servitude, obedience, and worship. More rare and confidential than these are the forms in which Divinity reduces the awe and reverence to enable sweeter and sweeter intimacy. The moniker "Krishna" indicates the Divinity who enables the apex of sweetness, intimacy, and confidentiality.

Divinity is the fountainhead of all ecstatic emotion - Krishna is the form of Divinity who facilitates *all* types of divine love, up to and

---

[1] *Bhagavad Gītā* 14.27

surpassing your wildest dreams of intimacy.[1] Thus Krishna is the *supreme* fountainhead, the *original* Divinity, "The Supreme Personality of Godhead."

Considering all our patent normalcy, however, you and I might honestly wonder if Krishna is "out of our league." First of all, he is beyond the substance of existence, but I certainly am not. So how will I even perceive him?

It is true that, on its own, a limited being cannot comprehend or perceive an unlimited being. The Divine, however, is truly unlimited. Thus the Divine can empower a limited being to directly perceive and comprehend him. We simply have to attract his interest to do so. We do so by expressing our desire to *really* love him. The more we cultivate and express this desire, the more the mystical energy of the divine becomes attracted to our being, gradually empowering our finitude to comprehend and interact with the infinitude of the all-blissful, all-attractive Divine.

---

[1] See, for example, *Bhāgavata Purāṇa* 10.43.17. "These women tasted Krishna as romance personified; these men experienced him as the supreme hero; those enemies thought him to be the crack of a thunderbolt."

To get divine love, therefore, is a miracle no less profound than seeing God face to face. It is possible only by the *empowerment* of Krishna's own energy. God's energy is as beginningless, endless, and self-causing as God himself. That is why Sanskrit scriptures describe divine love as "self-causing, and without the bounds of beginning and end."[1] It is not the effect of any cause. It cannot be generated or extinguished. It causes its own existence.

Although this sounds ultra-philosophical, it's also quite simple. We all know firsthand that even ordinary love can't be bought, forced, or manufactured. Only love creates love, and only divine love creates divine love.[2]

So, if I want divine love, I must find someone who has it. If I approach that person with a wide-open, receptive attitude, I will "catch" it, just like I catch a cold if I get very close to someone who already has one, or just like a stick catches fire when it's close to a stick that is already burning.

But, if I get it from you, and you got it from him, and he got it from her, and she got it from

---

[1] *Bhāgavata Purāṇa* 1.2.6 - *ahaituky apratihatā*
[2] *Bhāgavata Purāṇa* 11.3.31 - *bhaktyā sañjātayā bhaktyā*

the other one… what is the *original* cause of divine love?

I felt this was a question worthy of placing before Śrī Gurudev. So, I approached him, very confident in his realization, and asked, "What is the original cause of divine love?"

"What do *you* think?" He replied.

"Well," I answered. "When I look in *Bhāgavata Purāṇa* I consistently find one word in the answers."

"What word? *Yadṛcchayā?*" He asked.

"Yes!" I answered, thrilled to see the sharpness of his learning. Encouraged, I recited some of those quotes:

> *One attains divine love by chance (yadṛcchayā).*[1]
>
> *The miraculous energy of God manifests by chance (yadṛcchayā).*[2]
>
> *By chance (yadṛcchayā), one gains affection for hearing about me.*[1]

---

[1] *Bhāgavata Purāṇa* 11.20.11
[2] *Bhāgavata Purāṇa* 3.26.4

He let out a cryptic, "Hmmmm." And then asked, squinting, "So you think this word, *yadṛcchayā,* means *by chance*? What does this mean?"

"I'm not sure," I said. "Like, by good luck?"

"No." He answered calmly. "There is no such thing as luck - at least not in the way most people think of it. What people call 'luck' is really the systematic result of *karma.* Good *karma* brings good luck. Bad *karma* brings bad luck. So if divine love comes by a lucky chance, then *karma* is the ultimate cause. Do you feel that this is an acceptable proposition? Hardly! *Karma* is an aspect of the *material* world. Spiritual and limitless divine love cannot come from something material and limited."

"What if we take *karma* out of the picture?" I asked. "Maybe it is just 'luck' in the sense of 'blind chance?'"

He laughed. "'Blind chance,' you say? That's no answer! It's like a mother asking her child how the milk spilled and the child saying, 'It just *happened.*' It's no explanation at all. Try again."

---

[1] *Bhāgavata Purāṇa* 11.20.8

I thought for a while, "Can I get divine love by Krishna's Mercy?"

"OK" he nodded encouragingly. "That's not entirely incorrect. But what causes Krishna to be merciful and give someone divine love?"

I literally scratched my head. "Maybe Krishna's mercy is causeless?"

"Causeless?" He said the word like he had never heard it before. "What does *that* mean?"

I was surprised at the question, because I had heard him use the word *causeless* dozens of times. "Well," I said, "It means there is no direct cause motivating Krishna's decision to be merciful and give divine love to someone."

"Then, how is it different from blind chance?" He asked.

"There is a will involved," I suggested. "It's not just chance, its Krishna's freewill. Maybe people get divine love when Krishna *feels like* giving it to them?"

He looked at me sternly for a while, like I had said something insulting. "What sort of person do you think Krishna is!?" He finally said, with an obvious effort towards self-control. "Do you think he would *'feel like'* being merciful to some people, but not to others? And 'causelessly,' too: without even a good reason!? What partiality! What favoritism! What duality and illusion! A 'God' who can be covered by such illusions is hardly 'God' at all! Is that what you think of Krishna?"

"Well no," I stammered, "but Krishna kills demons and delights devotees. Doesn't that mean that in some ways he *is* partial?"

The guru laughed deeply. I was pretty relieved to hear that laugh, to tell you the truth. "The demons come to Krishna *looking for* a fight," He explained. "Krishna gives them what they want. The devotees come to him hoping to delight him. He gives them what they want, delighting them in the process. He gives everyone what they want, with absolute impartiality."

"Well," I blurted out, "If I can't get divine love from Krishna, where *can* I get it?!"

"It's not that it doesn't *come from* Krishna," he offered. "But Krishna is not the one deciding who gets it and who doesn't."

A new possibility sprang into my head and I expressed it right away, "What if Krishna gives divine love only to those who want it?"

"Good!" Gurudev exclaimed with a big smile. "Now you are thinking deeply! Now you are starting to understand the real meaning of '*yadṛcchayā!*' It does not mean *by chance*. That is merely a connotation from common use. The real root of the word is *icchā* - 'will, desire.' Divine love originates from God's *desire* and awaits the welcoming embrace of *your* desire. You have to *want* it before you get it.

"Now try to answer this," he continued, "Why does one person want it, while another doesn't?"

When a few moments passed without hint of an answer from me, he looked deeply into my eyes and asked, "Well, how did *you* start to want it?"

"I read a skateboarding magazine that had an article on an awesome band, who were devotees of Krishna."

I thought this would surprise him, but instead he exclaimed: "Exactly!!! You see?!?"

"Not really…"

"You don't see? *Only love can cause love*! You got devotion from devotees. You got your interest in divine love as a result of coming into contact with someone who had divine love. This is the answer to your question! Do you understand?"

"Sort of," I said. "But why did *I*, of all people, come in contact with devotees?"

He answered very deliberately, "Because... you... *wanted*... too." After letting the silence sink in, he finished up, "*yadṛcchayā*... 'by freewill'... *your* freewill. Many people read that magazine. How many became devotees as a result? Hmmm?"

"Probably only a few." I admitted.

"Perhaps only you!" He stressed. "Why? Because your desire was there, causing receptivity. That's why this article made you a devotee, but did not have that effect on everyone."

"But what was the cause of my will?" I asked, falling into a philosophical spiral.

"Don't be silly." He said, relaxing. "Don't lose touch with reality. Everyone knows that freewill is causeless." And a smile beamed from ear to ear, making him look almost like he was winking at me!

"So divine love comes from... will?"

"Yes!" He said with such relish, "Love is the purest, most exalted form of bliss, bliss is the purpose of existence, and God is the supreme existence, so God's will for ever-expanding divine love is always there. But, for some individuals like us, *our* will is not. Love, even God's infinite love, cannot force its way into us. Love cannot be forced! That is the very nature of love! It waits for your will to become receptive, *then* it descends to empower your heart and soul by putting you into contact with people who are already empowered."

"Then what is the role of *mercy?*" I asked.

"It is the devotee's mercy that they make themselves available to us materialistic fools. When a lover of Krishna speaks to us about their feelings for Krishna, they *share* their divine love with us. This is the real definition of "mercy" and it is the true conduit through which divine love begins! If your ear is open and willing to hear this mercy, the *seed* of divine love will enter your heart. Once you have that seed it is up to you to care for it and cultivate so it can bear its fullest fruit."

Other Paths to Divine Love?

As we spoke it drew closer to sunset and many other people had gradually come into the room. Śrī Gurudev took up *karatāla* (small hand-cymbals for keeping time) and began *nāma saṁkīrtan* (singing the names of Krishna).

Religion and Divine Love

Kīrtan went on sweetly and forcefully for almost an hour as still more people were drawn to assemble. When it finally came to a conclusion, a man dressed as a priest addressed Gurudev in a challenging tone of voice: "Why are you wasting everyone's time like this, chanting over and over and over again? If you really want to please God and get "divine love" you should get out of this room and go help people in need!"

The air then took to silence for a long time, as if to recover from the bruises of bearing these harsh words. At last, Gurudev replied humbly, quietly, and slowly: "How can *I* help anyone? What do I have that they truly need? Am I not also a beggar? As far as I know, the only item of any value I possess is my hope for divine love. So how can I really help anyone else except by sharing the wealth of this hope with them? Is that not exactly what I have tried to do, again and again - over and over - for the last hour?"

The priest was taken aback, but he was not ready to give up. "Chanting something over and over is not the right way to share divine love!" He said. "You are ignoring the principles of morality and religion and just sitting around chanting all day! How will that help at all?"

Gurudev sat up straighter and his eyes became sharper. "My friend," he asked, "are you saying that if I follow *your* idea of religion, *your* idea of morality, then I can gain the divine love I seek?"

"Yes!" The priest answered, confidently.

"No," countered the guru sharply, suddenly raising his voice. "Religion does *not* directly lead to divine love. It is an entirely different thing with an entirely different end result!"

A man sitting next to the priest spoke out, "But in church we pray to God, sing songs to glorify Him, and bow before Him. You do these same things! Why are you saying religion is so different from what you do?"

Gurudev answered. "Yes, *on the surface* it looks like you and I do many of the same things. There are two reasons for the apparent similarities between religion and divine love. The first is that only divine love has any true spiritual potency, and thus religion has no power without donning at least some of the trappings of divine love. The second is that divine love has no boundaries, and thus is free to express herself in any venue she chooses, including a church, mosque, or temple. Nonetheless, I really must try to impress upon you the fact that the *motives* of religion and divine love are diametrically different."

"How so?" The priest asked.

"What is your motive?" Gurudev replied. "Why do you bow to God? What do you hope to gain from your songs of praise? What do you ask for in your prayers?"

"Well, different people ask for different things." The priest answered.

"But you all ask for *something!*" Gurudev replied. "We do *not*. That is the crucial difference between religion and divine love! The pleasure of our beloved is the only thing we want from our prayers or songs or whatever seemingly 'religious' or 'non-religious' things we might do."

The priest had nothing to reply, so the Guru continued in a much more studious tone, directing his words more towards the entire audience. “The motive of an action is the most important factor determining its outcome. Since religion and divine love have very different motives they have very different outcomes. The result of being moral, doing good deeds, and praying is that you get good karma – pious merit – the opposite of ‘sin.’ That brings you ‘good luck’ and even takes you to ‘heaven’ to fulfill all the desires you repeatedly pestered God to cater to. All well and good, but my dear people please note, you have achieved the satisfaction of *your own* desires, a selfish thing! By no stretch of the imagination have you attained divine love in any way, shape or form!”

All were silent and thoughtful, so Gurudev continued. “What we do here, we do solely and purely with the heartfelt desire to please the divine. The result of such actions is the pleasure of the divine and the amplification of our mutual love for one another. It is imperative to acknowledge that *only love causes love.* Actions done out of divine love - out of singular desire to please the divine - only those actions will generate divine love, even if they do not appear religious at all. On the other hand, actions done out of a desire to please oneself, even if they appear religious, will never generate one iota of divine love!"

In a softened voice the priest asked, "Then what is the real purpose of religion?"

"If divine love is a flame," said the guru, "and the soul is wood, then religion and morality are like wind and sunlight - helping to dry the wood out, evaporating the moisture of selfishness, so that it can ignite more easily when in contact with divine love."

Everyone appreciated the analogy.

Gurudev continued: "Why does the divine incarnate in the world? Some say he wants to remove demonic forces from the world.[1] But there is a deeper reason: he wants to manifest his beautiful name, form, qualities and pastimes so that new souls can have the fortune of being attracted to divine love![2] Similarly, people think God wants them to be religious. Does he? Maybe, but only insofar as it facilitates making them more

---

[1] See *Bhagavad Gītā* 4.8

[2] (*Bhāgavata Purāṇa* 4.8.47 and similarly in 10.14.2), "God conducts his appearance and activities due to his own desire."

amenable to the beauty of divine love. Do you understand?"

"Yes," said the priest, visibly moved. "So should I give up my religion?"

"You should give up your own selfish motivations, your ambitions for selfish rewards like heaven and good karma. There is no need to give up your religion. Keep doing what you are doing, but do it only for the sake of pleasing the divine and for no other reward. Then you will transcend 'religion' and enter the arena of divine love, which will generate more and more divine love.[1] Know for certain that any deed, however 'religious' it may appear, can never generate divine love if it is motivated by something other than the desire to please the divine."[2]

He stretched out his arms and called for me to hand him the *Bhāgavata Purāṇa*, the essence of *Vedānta* and thus the most evolved of all Sanskrit spiritual and philosophical tomes. Turning through its pages he read aloud the following:

---

[1] *Bhāgavata Purāṇa* 10.47.24
[2] *Bhāgavata Purāṇa* 11.12.9

If a person gains love for Krishna, but fails in every religious duty - he loses nothing. If a person fulfills every religious duty, but achieves no real love for Krishna - he gains nothing.[1]

Then, flipping to the other end of the large book he read:

Philosophy without divine love is nothing but hard work, like beating an empty husk of rice.[2]

Again flipping back to the other side of the book…

In the past many yogis became frustrated with their difficult practices and simply turned to you for shelter. As a result of this devotional attitude they very quickly and easily gained what was so frustrating and difficult to attain through yoga and meditation alone.[3]

"You see," he looked up to explain, "Divine love is the essence and ultimate purpose of all paths for

---

[1] *Bhāgavata Purāṇa* 1.5.17
[2] *Bhāgavata Purāṇa* 10.14.4
[3] *Bhāgavata Purāṇa* 10.14.5

evolving the human spirit. Therefore every path *requires* an element of *bhakti* to become successful. Divine love, on the other hand, is completely self-sufficient. It does not need assistance from religion or anything else!"

He then dove again into quoting from the *Purāṇa*:

> *Everything possible to attain through sacrifice, austerity, logical reasoning, and renunciation easily comes to my devotees as a result of their devotion."*[1]

> *The most holy person is one who ignores all religion and simply loves me wholeheartedly.*[2]

"And this should remind you of the famous conclusion of *Bhagavad Gītā*: '*Abandon all religion and just surrender your heart to me.*'[3] " Then, returning to his book he flipped through the pages to read another quote:

---

[1] *Bhāgavata Purāṇa* 11.20.32-33
[2] *Bhāgavata Purāṇa* 11.11.32
[3] *Bhagavad Gītā* 18.65

One who loves me has nothing left to gain from logic or renunciation.[1]

Looking up from the book, like a man looking up from a delicious meal, he said, "Why is it that all other paths need divine love? Because without the divine beloved, all I have is myself and my own strength. Without the empowering mercy of the divine beloved, I have to do everything *perfectly* at the proper time, in the proper place, with the proper materials, in the proper cleanliness, and after having proper qualifications. That is why Śrīdhara Swāmī writes…" Grabbing another book from the shelf above his head, he flipped to a page and read:

If a mantra is incomplete, mispronounced, or pronounced at the wrong moment its meaning changes and can become as disastrous and destructive as a thunderbolt.[2]

"Divine love is not like this!" He nearly shouted with enthusiasm. "Nothing is more powerful than divine love! No imperfection can block it or restrict it in the least!" Again picking up the

---

1 *Bhāgavata Purāṇa* 11.20.31
2 Sridhar Swami quote this verse from *Paniniya-Shiksha* in his commentary on *Bhagavat Purāṇa* 6.9.11

Purāṇa, he eagerly and deftly paged to the following, which he read aloud with delight:

> *O hunter! There are no rules or prohibitions on who can chant the names of Hari, nor on where or when it is appropriate or inappropriate.*[1]

> *Just a single utterance of Krishna's name will deliver any human being from the cycle of birth and death, even if it is just said carelessly.*[2]

Someone in the room then asked, "Guru Jī , You say nothing can block divine love... What about lust? Doesn't lust and selfishness block divine love?"

"Lust does not *block* divine love," the guru answered, "it is simply the *absence* of divine love. Still, I agree, it does act like an obstacle for all practical purposes. What is unique about divine love, though, is that that she will not be overcome by this obstacle. Divine love herself, without any outside help, will destroy the obstacle of selfish

---

[1] "*Vaishnava Smriti*"
[2] *Hari-bhakti-vilasa* 11.451

lust! Surely you know this quote," and then he recited from memory:

> *Anyone who affectionately hears about the loving affairs between Krishna and his Gopi girlfriends loses all lusty desires.*[1]

"Or you must know this famous statement from the *Gītā*:"

> *A person who practices unalloyed devotion to me is saintly, even if they might still do something selfish and lustful as a result of their flaws.*[2]

Then he paged through the book for another quote, to explain the *Gītā* passage he just recited:

> *My* bhakta *might not yet be able to restrain his senses from the objects of enjoyment, but he is never completely overwhelmed by illusion. This is because of the power of his love for me.*[3]

"And of course," Gurudev said, "You all must know the story of Ajāmila, no? He affectionately

---

[1] *Bhāgavata Purāṇa* 10.33.40
[2] *Bhagavad Gītā* 9.30
[3] *Bhāgavata Purāṇa* 11.14.18

called the name of God, 'Nārāyaṇa', but maybe it was only because he named his son 'Nārāyaṇa'. Obviously he wasn't properly practicing devotion, but still the messengers of Nārāyaṇa and Yamarāja agreed that he was not subject to normal laws of *karma.* This shows that divine love can bear significant fruits even if we don't do it correctly!

"So, no," Gurudeva concluded, "not even selfish lusts can permanently block divine love."

Knowledge and Divine Love

One of the guru's students then asked, "Gurudev, you say that divine love will overcome all flaws, and it doesn't even have to be practiced *correctly*?"

The guru began to laugh heartily, saying, "Right! That's right! But, that doesn't mean I *should* practice it incorrectly! It means that *even if* I make mistakes or get things wrong, *bhakti*[1] *herself* corrects me and sets me right. She does not heartlessly penalize me."

---

[1] *Bhakti* is a Sanskrit term for "divine love."

"But Gurudev," the student continued to inquire, "it seems like there are so many things to learn, so many books to study..."

"Certainly when you love someone there is so much to learn about them!" The guru said. "But, such study is an act of love, not an intellectual summersault! We have nothing against intellectualism, but it is foolish to say that intellectual discipline is a mandatory requirement for advancement on the path of *bhakti*! Divine love is beyond even the ultimate goal of intellectual discipline: enlightenment." Then he reached again for the *Purāṇa*:

> *Krishna grants enlightenment without thinking twice, but rarely does he give bhakti.*[1]

> *Even among millions of enlightened intellectuals you will be lucky to find one soul who is truly happy, due to having bhakti.*[2]

Another student now asked, "If this is true, what is the use of the logical and scientific portions of

---

[1] *Bhāgavata Purāṇa* 5.6.18
[2] *Bhāgavata Purāṇa* 6.14.5

our Sanskrit scripture? Or what is the use of scientific thinking?"

Showing no signs of tiring in the least, the Śrī Guru answered. "Just because something is imperfect doesn't mean it is absolutely useless."

Before he could fully explain this idea, someone else interrupted to ask, "Why do you say that logic and science is imperfect?"

Gurudev answered, "Science, the mechanism of advancement on the intellectual path, relies on accurate observation. Is it not?"

"Certainly," the man replied, "that is the foundation of all empiric sciences."

"Alright," Gurudev continued. "The ability to make accurate observations, however, relies on the clarity of my senses, which is a result of the clarity of my mind and intellect, which is all determined by the purity of my ego. Every bit of empiric data must pass through the lens of my ego before it reaches my consciousness. If my ego is not pure, my perception of reality will be distorted. Conclusions based on distorted observations are imperfect - this is a basic scientific principle in itself, you have confirmed, right? So, those who follow the path of knowledge must also strive to purify their ego. If not, their science will often come to disastrous results, as was the case in ancient Indian history with Kaṁsa, Rāvaṇa, and Hiraṇyakaśipu, and is also obvious in modern history by the invention of atomic bombs and so forth. The scientific path leads to an auspicious destination only if the person treading that path has purified their ego."

"How does one purify the ego?" The man asked, eagerly.

"That is the purpose of *religion*!" Gurudev said, gesturing towards the priest. "Religion engages people in selfless acts for the benefit of others. This purifies our ego of most of its major defects and qualifies us to graduate from the path of religion to the spiritual path of science. The path of religion however, is very difficult to navigate without divine love, as I mentioned before. Since spiritual science is founded on the path of religion, it is twice as difficult to navigate without divine love. In all pursuits on all paths, we have to take shelter of divine love if we want anything better than astronomical odds of success."

"Gurujī," an older lady at the back of the room called out, "why do many people give quotes from scripture saying that divine love is just an inferior component of religion and philosophy? Is this true?"

"It is not really true, but there is no harm in letting them say it." The guru answered. "After all, Viṣṇu[1] did once appear as a *dwarf*, right? He became the *younger* brother of Indra. He took a subordinate position to this ordinary demigod because he is compassionate and wants to be helpful. Divine love is even more compassionate than God, so of course she accepts subordinate roles assisting the paths of religion and knowledge. Without her aid, practically no one on these other paths would ever gain success. So there is no harm in such statements, however narrow their focus may be.

"You see," he continued, "Divine love is *all-powerful*. She can grant any boon, but nothing else can grant her as a boon! She can create anything, but nothing can create her! She is self-creating, self-sustaining. She is as great as God! In a sense she is greater than God, for she has the power to delight and fascinate God! To get divine love in

---

[1] A name for the Supreme Being playing a somewhat active role in the mundane world.

my own heart is the supreme goal I could ever hope to strive for. I think it's the supreme goal *anyone* could ever hope to strive for. And what is the path to achieve that supreme goal? There is no other direct path *except* divine love! Divine love is the supreme means to the supreme goal!"

Suddenly the guru became dejected and morose, and began to quietly weep. Everyone's mood fell through the floor in response. "Gurudev, what's wrong?" Someone asked.

"If I know all these things," he replied softly, "why do I hold on stubbornly to other paths and other goals? I am like a foolish animal that constantly needs to be herded towards the correct path! ...Let's speak no more. Let's sing the names of our beloved Krishna together, and give one another strength."

With that we again began *Hari-nāma-saṁkīrtana* well into the night.

Chapter Two

The First Three Steps

Once upon an extraordinarily fortunate time, curiosity took me into the company of people who carried divine love in their hearts. By contact with them, a priceless seed-germ was planted in the soil of my own heart. This seed was an idea: "Don't seek happiness independently, find it within the pleasure of The Divine! You are running endless circles chasing your own pleasure. Stop. Chase the pleasure of The Divine, and happiness will chase *you*!"

This idea spread its roots through my heart and mind. I became like a gardener, sprinkling this seed with the water of sincere affection for All-Attractive Krishna. Quickly, the rooted seed became a vine that climbed throughout my mind and spread her branches into all my senses. Her touch, like alchemy, transformed my entire being from the iron of selfish materialism to the molten gold of pure spirituality. Eventually, I became like a bumblebee thirsty to make honey from the pollen of those flowers, thirsty to relish the ecstatic experience of the divine loving affairs of All-Attractive Krishna.

But, first things first: let's start from the beginning and proceed step by step.

The Two Initial Qualities of Divine Love

As soon as the vine of divine love emerged from the soil of my heart, two leaves begin to unfurl. At first I could only see the bottom of these leaves, because the tops were still furled up towards the stalk. Those bottoms are regulated by King Vaidhi.[1] Appreciating his kingdom, I used the logic and authority of scripture and morality as an inspiration to seek divine love.

Before long, however, I caught a glimpse of the unfurling leaf-tops. The kingdom there is run by King Rāga.[2] It was even more attractive, shiny, smooth, and beautiful than the rough bottoms! *Much* more! Enchanted by this beauty, I began to

---

[1] *Vaidhi* means "from injunctions."
[2] *Rāga* means "from passion."

pursue divine love not out of intellect or ethics, but out of passion for it.

The shade of each leaf produces its own effect. As they unfurl in unison, the shade of one extinguishes all my suffering. The shade of the other grants me everything auspicious.

Thus it is said:

> *Divine love simultaneously brings auspiciousness and destroys inauspiciousness.*[1]

Uprooting Suffering

Ignorance is the root cause of all suffering. Ignorance of who and what I really am causes me to embrace an illusion of "self" within the phantasmagoria of the material world. This causes suffering because it subjects me to the fearsome material timeline, which spirals inexorably to death.

This is not the only suffering created by ignorance. There is another, more constant suffering. When I ignore the fact that I am a

---

[1] *Bhāgavata Purāṇa* 11.2.42

functional part of The Divine, I embrace the untruth that I am an independent entity. This puts a self-centered focus on my natural desires. Then, by acting on those selfish desires I become subject to their repercussions, thus setting the huge wheel of *karma* in motion.

Karma is a weed that corrupts the soil of the heart. Its root is *ignorance* - the catalyst of a false sense of self, independent from The Divine. Its stalk is made from *selfish attitudes*, and produces branches: *selfish desires*. These branches produce leaves: *selfish actions,* the repercussions of which are the fruits and flowers of the weed. The flowers are *unmanifest repercussions* - waiting for the birds and bees of destiny to bring it to fruition. The fruits, some bitter some sweet, are *manifest repercussions* that create the tangible conditions of our material life.[1]

Divine love roots out the original cause of this complex and miserable chain reaction by replacing ignorance with knowledge – knowledge

---

[1] The technical terminology for these six stages of suffering are: *avidyā* (ignorance), *kūṭa* ("the first thing to appear" - selfish attitudes), *bīja* ("the seed" - selfish desires), *karma* ("deeds" - selfish actions), *aprārabdha-karma* (unmanifest repercussions of deeds), *prārabdha-karma* (manifest repercussions of deeds).

that my self-interest lies only in the divine beloved, that his pleasure alone is my pleasure, and that my identity has true substance only within him.

Establishing Auspiciousness

The root of auspiciousness is the loss of interest in selfish pleasure and gain of interest in the divine pleasure of Godhead. From this root springs all other good qualities like mercy, forgiveness, truthfulness, peacefulness, gravity, respect, humility, etc.

The two leaves of divine love unfold gradually while the vine grows toward full flowering. This growth passes nine stages, beginning with *conviction.*

Conviction[1]

When I began cultivating the seed of divine love, the first thing I noticed was that my *conviction*

---

[1] Ś*raddhā*

began to change. I had always been convinced that fulfilling my own desires would make me happy and content, but now I started to doubt this and instead entertain the idea that trying to please God would make me more content and happy. At first I merely considered this idea casually, from time to time, as a result of circumstances. Gradually, however, it grew into a heartfelt curiosity too fascinating not to pursue.

Guidance[1]

As my conviction in the value of divine love increased, I became more eager to seek it. For this I needed guidance, at least a pointer in the right direction. So I began to search for people who had some experience with this sort of thing. Eventually I found a few particularly helpful people to guide me.

What makes a guide truly "helpful"? First of all they had to be more experienced than me (not hard to find, to tell you the truth). Second, they just had to *like* me (and vice versa). Third, the "*mood*" of their divine love had to be harmonious

---

[1] *Sādhu-saṅga*

with the mood I was interested in. There are infinite varieties of divine love; I needed guides with experience cultivating the specific variety that I was attracted to.

The generous goddess of divine love sent me many such helpful guides. Soon, one among them really stood out and became my primary *guru*. Headed by him, many *gurus* became my guidance-system on the quest for divine love. These *gurus* continued to put me in contact with more *gurus*. With all this expanding guidance, I began to get a clearer understanding of divine love in an application that was immediate and *practical* to me.

Practice[1]

I eventually began put all their guidance into practice. At first, this was but a flash of momentary inspiration, but gradually I became deep, serious, and steady about practicing divine love.

---

[1] *Bhajana-kriyā*

I could not begin really concentrating on deep and steady practice until I evolved through six distinct phases of superficial and unsteady practice:

(1) Initial enthusiasm

(2) Mood swings

(3) Indecision

(4) Struggle with sense gratification

(5) Struggle with devotional practices

(6) Exploitation of devotion

Initial Enthusiasm[1]

Starting to learn a new subject is exciting; we are full of optimism, mostly because we don't yet know enough about the subject to realize how little we know! Thus, at the very beginning of devotional practice, I was carried along by an initial rush of enthusiasm, not knowing enough about divine love to even realize how small my first steps were and how far I was from the ultimate goal.

[1] *Utsāha-mayī*

Mood Swings[1]

Soon enough, though, my extreme distance from the goal started to dawn on me. I had to face the truth that I took up an extremely deep subject that would take serious and prolonged effort to master. Whenever I mustered the courage to face this fact, it dampened my enthusiasm, discouraging my effort to practice divine love.

Being immature and having no other recourse, I would compensate for these depressing "doubts" by trying to pour on more childish enthusiasm. The result is that I came into a stage of extreme "mood swings" in my practice. Eventually, the exhaustion of these forced me to confront my extreme distance from the divine goal with more mature realism.

Indecision[2]

Confronting my lack of qualifications for divine love opened Pandora 's Box of indecision. I thought:

> *"It's looking more and more like it's going to take a herculean effort to attain divine love…*

---

[1] *Ghana-taralā*
[2] *Vyūḍha-vikalpā*

Should I make that effort, or just give up and wait for another lifetime or something?"

Eventually I decided I should go for it. But how?

"Should I abandon everything and run off to sacred Vṛndāvana to practice without distraction? Well, yes, but can I really get free from distractions just by running away from them? Well, no, so shouldn't I just be patient and wear out all my material desires by living a normal, fulfilling social life while practicing devotion? Well, probably, but then why do so many practitioners describe the comforts of home as something dire to be dropped like the plague?"

I passed many weeks and months perplexed by the mazes of these questions and answers that only raise more questions. Eventually, I made up my mind:

"If I die with unsatisfied material desires I will have to be reborn to fulfill them, so why not fulfill them now in some reasonable manner that does not totally distract from my humble practice of divine love? Then, when I am truly ready, I will really go to Vṛndāvana

and exclusively worship Krishna day and night without distraction."

But this soon turned out to be much more difficult than I imagined.

"I am struggling day and night with responsibilities towards my family. Meanwhile, renunciates wander here and there, carefree. As the saying goes, 'wherever the renunciate went, there was plenty of lunch.' It would be easier to fulfill my material desires in the garb of a renunciate! But what hypocrisy that would be!"

During this phase of indecision such battles constantly raged in my mind, and many others, too… What service should I do for the divine? How? Where?? When???

Struggle with Sense Gratification[1]

After being perplexed and derailed for what felt like a very long time, I came to realize that the external details of life are not very important. What is important is that, *whatever* external situation I am in, I give up the inner mentality of

---

[1] *viṣaya-saṅgarā*

being the subject of pleasure, and instead adopt the mentality of being an object meant to please the divine.

Viṣṇu Purāṇa says:

> *Sense gratification is in one direction and divine love is in the other.*

I came to realize that "sense gratification" wasn't just an external affair; it was a state of mind - the state of mind that is exactly opposite from divine love. My quest for divine love did not necessitate external changes so much as it demanded internal revolution, from the consciousness of being the subject for objects of sense gratification to the consciousness of myself becoming an object to please the divine subject. My war with indecision reached a truce when I stopped second-guessing my external conditions and started focusing my internal mentality.

Well... "Give up the inner mood of sense gratification." That was easier said than done! I would succeed at weeding one corner of my heart's garden only to find the same weeds pop up in another, sometimes twice as strong! Yet I was sincerely trying, and feeling humble about my repeated failures.

Struggle with Devotional Practices[1]

Sooner or later I realized why it was so difficult to protect the garden of my heart from the weeds of sense gratification: It is very hard to get rid of lower mentalities without attaining higher mentalities. To push out the weeds I needed to plant more flowers. I needed to experience something better than selfish gratification.

So I entered the fifth phase of devotional practice: trying to fill my life with more and more sincere devotional activities. I made plans like, "I will chant more, such and such number of rounds every day." Or, "I will bow to a certain number of *bhaktas* every day, and serve them." Or, "I will speak only about Krishna's name, form, qualities and pastimes and will flee from all other conversations."

Wonderful plans, right? The hard part was following through.

Exploitation of Devotion[2]

It was impossible at first, but with continued effort, I gradually began to succeed and practice devotion fairly seriously. This is when people first

---

[1] *Niyamākṣamā*

[2] *Taraṅga-raṅgiṇī*

started saying, “Hey, you are a pretty special guy!” And so began my sixth phase: Exploitation of Devotion.

Nothing is as beautiful and attractive as divine love. Thus, no one is more beautiful and attractive than a divine lover. Even the first successful steps towards divine love make one quite attractive, and naturally popular. Popularity brings power, and that’s… tempting.

At this stage I suddenly found a lot of people sort of just waiting on my doorstep, tempting my ego - which was quite susceptible to such temptation because the truth is I was still a beginner, still very selfish at heart. In small, innocent increments, I fell prey to exploiting these resources for my own agendas, needs, and whims - and my progress towards divine love took a U-turn.

It was very difficult to get past this phase. I had to become so sincere in my desire to please Krishna that any popularity resulting as a side effect didn’t catch my interest, or if it did, seemed repulsively dangerous to my real goals. The weakness of enjoying selfish benefits from divine love is like odorous garbage polluting a flower garden. Developing the sincerity to detox the heart from such pollution often requires a lot of hard-knocks on the road to purity. Thus, upon arriving at this sixth phase of initial practice, we must set our focus clearly on the next stage of development: purification.

Chapter Three

Impurities[1]

Selfishness is the ultimate impurity, the absolute antithesis to true selfless devotion. Selfishness manifests four primary effects:

1. Attempts to avoid suffering

2. Attempts to attain pleasure

3. Attempts to do the above, but masked in the context of "selfless devotion"

4. Lack of interest in, or even derisiveness towards, the elements of selfless devotion.

The first two effects concern the good and bad results of *karma*. These two are not really all that serious in the bigger picture, because devotional

---

[1] *Anartha-nivṛtti*

practice purifies them relatively quickly. The third, exploiting the side effects of devotion, is more difficult to overcome at first - but triumph rather soon comes suddenly and quite completely. The fourth branch of selfishness, however - disinterest and derisiveness towards the elements of selfless love - *by far* manifests the most pernicious and persistent impurities.

The most serious of these are offenses towards the saintly, offenses towards the gods, offenses towards scriptures, and intentional wrongdoing.

Offending the Saintly

This is the worst of the worst of the worst impurities. As discussed the worst impurity is offensiveness towards elements of devotion. The most important element of devotion is the holy name of Krishna. Therefore, offensiveness towards the Name is the worst of the worst impurities. Of all offenses to Krishna's name, denigration of the Name's chanter is the worst of the worst of the worst of impurities. *Nothing* blocks the progress of genuine divine love and crushes that sacred flower with more fearsome vengeance than animosity towards those who dedicate themselves to Krishna's name.

I may say that I have no such enmity towards devotees of the holy name, but if I stand before you without divine love overflowing from my heart, you know I am (at best) just fooling myself. If you have a fever, we know you have an infection. Similarly if I lack pure divine love, you know I still harbor dislike towards devotees of Krishna's name.

To feel unloving towards someone who is trying to develop love for Krishna is the most terrible and tenacious impurity blocking me from realizing divine love. To express these ill feelings verbally (let's not even mention physical expressions of ill-will) is *extremely* destructive. It is like a wild and enraged elephant trampling a garden.

How can I cure these offenses? By feeling genuine sorrow for them and expressing that sorrow in ways that warrant true forgiveness. Like this:

"Why am I repulsed by people who are trying to be saintly? What is wrong with me!? And I don't even have the basic manners to contain these disgusting feelings; instead I blurt them out as rude insults! I wish I was not like this!!!" With this realization of regret I approached those I had offended and sincerely apologized.

Some easily forgave me, but others were not impressed. I realized, "Wow, I insulted this person so much more deeply than my huge, blinding ego would let me recognize! I will have to express my apology with deeper sincerity and practicality. Hopefully then they will forgive me."

Some then forgave, but a few remained unmoved. I realized, "I am going to have to suffer the effects of those deep insults for a long, long time. All I can do is keep trying to apologize, and take full shelter of my devotional practices - headed by *nāma sankīrtan*[1] - to purify my heart from making similar blunders in the future."

It was not easy to think like that. Every fiber in my self-serving heart was protesting, "God, what the hell is wrong with this moron? I am humbling myself and asking for forgiveness again and again, but this egomaniac still won't forgive me??? Bah! What kind of 'saint' is she? If she was *really* all

---

[1] Singing the names of Krishna in a group, especially the names: *Hare Krishna, Hare Krishna, Krishna Krishna, Hare Hare Hare Rama, Hare Rama, Rama Rama, Hare Hare.*

that 'saintly' she wouldn't have taken this insult so seriously to begin with." Luckily, I knew enough to recognize these thoughts as the gigantic plate-mail armor of egoistic non-devotion, so I tried to ignore them.

I couldn't. My ego-serving intellect kept arguing, "How can you say he is a 'saint'? Look what he did to you, and to others!!! How is it an 'offense' to point out what a cheater this man is!?! 'Call a spade a spade.' If he was truly a 'saint' you would have nothing ill to point out in the first place!"

To combat the ogre of this argument requires a sharp, clear-cut definition of "saintly." The *Padma Purāṇa* gives this definition:

> *People who behave poorly - who are fallen, deceitful, egotistical, bodily conscious, drunk, cruel, irreligious, uncultured, mean, greedy, attached and illusioned - are actually saints, if they merely take shelter of Govinda's feet.*[1]

I had to deeply comprehend authoritative statements like these to bravely and unyieldingly accept the fact that a saint can have thousands of

---

[1] *Padma Purāṇa* 4.25.9, quoted in *Hari Bhakti Vilas* 11.655

defects.[1] If I want to really progress towards realizing divine love I must not criticize a person who takes shelter of Govinda, even if that person behaves very poorly.[2] Who, then, could possibly calculate the absolutely disastrous impact of criticizing those who are highly elevated souls possessing abundant qualities of humility, tolerance, mercy, truthfulness, etc.? The cataclysmic effect of feeling and expressing non-loving emotions towards such personalities cannot be described. To say it is like an atomic bomb exploding on a tender flower would be an understatement.

You may ask, "But such persons are so full of saintly qualities that they almost never feel offended by any insult. Doesn't this mean it is very difficult or even impossible to offend them?"

Yes, but Bhāgavata says:

> *The dust of the feet of such great souls blocks the progress of offenders.*[3]

---

[1] See also, *Bhagavad Gītā* 9.30, *api cet sudurācāro…*
[2] If you are wondering, "Then who will correct the person?" - see Appendix A: Notes, If I Don't Criticize You, Who Will?
[3] *Bhāgavata Purāṇa* 4.4.13

This means that although a very elevated saint never personally takes offense, things *connected to* the saint ("dust of the feet") *do*. To put it plainly, the many followers and admirers of that saint will all be offended and this will block my progress *multiple* times. If I insult someone who does not feel insulted by what I said or did, it is *worse* than insulting someone who does become upset! I should immediately and attentively beg forgiveness from such humble and tolerant saints, *and their followers*. Failing this, the gulf between divine love and my heart will be more insurmountable that the intergalactic distances of deep space.

Hearing how dangerous it is to offend the saintly devotees, you may think it safer to keep your distance from them. But please remember that the second step towards divine love is the intimate association of saintly devotees! If you abandon their association in fear of offending them, you will not progress. Therefore, even if you are committing offenses, do not stray from the valuable company of the saintly. Stay with them and seek the safety of constant apology and humility.

Saintly devotees very often give magnanimous blessings even towards undeserving offenders. Here are some historical examples:

1. Jaḍa Bharata blessed King Rahūgaṇa even after the king drafted him into slave-like labor and viciously belittled and insulted him.

2. Uparicara Vasu blessed the demons who came to kill him when he retired from battle to do his devotional practices.

3. Nityānanda Prabhu blessed Madhai even after Madhai struck him violently on the forehead.

Offending the Gods

After offending the lovers of Krishna, the next worst blockade to divine love is to offend the gods. I wind up offending the gods if I don't clearly understand the relative positions of all living beings, especially Viṣṇu and Śiva.

There are two overarching-categories of living beings: 1. independent, and 2. dependent. Independent beings are self-causing and self-sustaining. Dependent beings, however, manifest from and rely on others. Independent beings are divine manifestations of Godhead. Dependent beings are everyone else.

There are two types of independent beings: 1. those who consort with illusion by directly interacting with material affairs, and 2. those who do not. Śiva and his expansions are manifestations of Godhead in direct contact with material affairs. Viṣṇu and his expansions are manifestations of Godhead without direct connection to material affairs.

> *Śiva's consort is Māyā, the illusory material energy. Through intimate relations with her, Śiva creates three types of ego influenced by her three aspects.*[1]

Although Śiva directly contacts material illusion, he is still an independent being, like Viṣṇu.

> *Yogurt is milk that has contacted bacteria. Still, it is essentially milk. Śiva is Govinda in intimate contact with material illusion. Still he is essentially an independent Godhead, like Govinda.*[2]

---

[1] *Bhāgavata Purāṇa* 10.88.3
[2] *Brahma Samhita* 5.45

Śiva is essentially the same as Viṣṇu, but he contacts the "bacteria" of illusion so he is not the most appropriate object of adoration for those with goals that are beyond the realm of illusion. Viṣṇu is the more appropriate object for divine adoration beyond all touch of illusion.

Besides Śiva there are other gods. Particularly important among them is Brahmā.

> *Godhead accepts three forms - Brahma, Viṣṇu, and Śiva - to create, maintain, and destroy the material universe.*[1]

When scripture mentions the three primary gods in the same breath like this, it is easy to feel that they are all in the same category. But this is a mistake. Brahmā himself explains:

> *The Sun can gift a portion of its radiance to a crystal held up to it. This is analogous to how I am empowered by the independent Godhead, Govinda.*[2]

Brahmā is a dependent being temporarily empowered by the independent Godhead. Some

---

[1] *Bhāgavata Purāṇa* 1.2.23
[2] *Brahma Samhita* 5.49

scriptures describe Viṣṇu and Brahmā as equals, to demonstrate the absolute efficacy of this empowerment.

There is a Brahma, Viṣṇu, and Śiva in *every* universe – and there are infinite universes. A highly evolved dependent being takes the post of Brahmā, but sometimes when there is no qualified soul, Viṣṇu expands to become Brahmā. This is another reason why scripture occasionally describes Brahmā and Viṣṇu as equal.

The trio of gods, Viṣṇu, Śiva, and Brahma, are parallel to the trio of primary qualities of material nature.

God	**Role**	**Quality**
Viṣṇu	Maintain the substance of the universe.	*Sattva* Clarity
Śiva	Destroy the universe	*Tamas* Darkening
Brahmā	Create the universe	*Rajas* Reddening

Thus each of the three gods works with a particular aspect of material nature. Viṣṇu provides and maintains the substances that

Brahma uses to create and which Śiva then destroys. Viṣṇu therefore is not directly active in the material nature.

The other two gods directly interact with material energy. Brahma deals with the creative energy, *rajas*, which "reddens" him. And Śiva deals with the destructive energy, *tamas*, which "darkens" him. Viṣṇu, on the other hand, remains clear (*sattva*). Therefore he alone is a god equal in stature to the original Independent Being who is transcendent to illusion.

The mode of clarity is superior to the reddening mode, which is superior to the darkening mode. So we might assume that Brahmā, the god of reddening energy, is superior to Śiva, the god of darkening energy. This would be a mistake. Bhāgavata explains why:

> *Smoke is superior to wood, and fire is superior to smoke. Similarly the reddening energy is superior to the darkening energy, and the clear energy is superior to the reddening energy.*[1]

---

[1] See *Bhāgavata Purāṇa* 1.2.24

In this metaphor, *fire* is clearly supreme. It represents the clear energy, and thus Viṣṇu. Smoke represents the dusty-reddish energy, and thus Brahmā. Wood represents the darkening energy, and thus Śiva. Fire can be produced from wood, but not from smoke! Smoke is merely a byproduct of fire, but in wood, fire *exists* in a potential state. This is why Śiva is superior to Brahmā, despite dealing with an inferior mode of material energy.

Moving our focus to the dependent beings, there are two types: those covered by illusion and those who are not. Among those not covered by illusion there are those who are empowered by Godhead, and those who are not. Among those who are empowered, there are two purposes: to help others become liberated from illusion - for example: the Four Kumāra, and to help others exist prosperously within illusion, for example: Brahmā.

Those liberated dependent beings not empowered by Godhead for some specific function in relation to illusion are of two types: those who have no individuality - who only *potentially* exist within the spiritual substance, and those who do have individuality and exist in a personal relationship with the transcendent Independent Being.

All types of living beings, from microbes to Godhead, fall into the above categories. Understanding these categories clearly is what saved me from falling victim to offensive attitudes similar to:

- "Only Viṣṇu is Godhead, not Śiva! I don't even want to see a temple of Śiva!"
- "Śiva is the only Godhead, not Viṣṇu! Why should I even look at Viṣṇu!?"
- "Any god will do."
- "I am as good as God!"

These offensive attitudes are very serious because the gods are saintly beings. Thus an offense to the gods is an offense to the saintly. Viṣṇu and Śiva are superlatively magnanimous and therefore rarely feel offended by anyone, but their saintly followers are more sensitive to offenses - which blocks our progress towards divine love.

Engaging in devotional practice, especially *nāma-saṁkīrtan*, with the correct understanding of the relative positions of Viṣṇu, Śiva, and Brahma will quickly cause the effects of this offense to disappear.

Offending the Scriptures

Most scripture and other sources of knowledge don't directly speak about pure divine love for Śrī Krishna. This does not mean, however, that such scriptures and sciences are useless and fit for denigration! They all serve an essential purpose: they facilitate practical, mental, emotional, and philosophical evolution for the masses, who are simply not yet ready to take a direct interest in divine love.

All knowledge eventually leads to self-realization, which itself culminates at the threshold of divine love. If I belittle any source of knowledge then I am belittling something that eventually leads to divine love. This attitude would impede my own quest for that divine love.

To rectify this offense, I should speak positively of the eventual link between sciences, religion and divine love. With this humble attitude towards all things that even indirectly lead to divine, I can very effectively engage in *nāma-saṁkīrtan* in the company of saintly people.

Intentionally Doing Wrong

Offending the saintly, the gods, and the scriptures are the three most significant impurities impeding the progress of divine love. There are others,[1] less virulent than these. Although they are easily overcome by the powerful effect of *nāma-saṁkīrtan,* I shouldn't be intentionally slack about them! To employ *nāma-saṁkīrtan* in this way - as a facilitator of my own laziness or neglect - is selfish. Thus it poses a significant block on the progress of divine love.

It is *not* an offense to make honest mistakes that one regrets and tries to atone for by *nāma-saṁkīrtan.* Nor is it an offense to disregard certain aspects of *bhakti* as a result of enthusiasm for *nāma-saṁkīrtan*. Evidence to this effect:

---

[1] See, for example, the 32 *sevāparādhā* mentioned in *Padma-Purāṇa.*

Chanting the ten-syllable mantra grants all perfection in divine love, without need for doing anything else.[1]

It is also said, in Bhāgavata:

Anyone who takes to the path of divine love, even if his knowledge of it is incomplete, will easily attain self-realization. Even if he runs on this path with his eyes closed he will not slip or fall.[2]

"Closing my eyes" means deliberately ignoring things. "Running" means to rush forward without going step by step, skipping over some parts of the path. Being blind to some things and skipping over them *out of enthusiasm to please Krishna in a certain way* (particularly, by *nāma-saṁkīrtan*) is certainly *not* an offense. Ignoring the need to please Krishna or being inattentive to doing so *is* antithetical to divine love, but ignoring some ways of pleasing him as a result of attentive enthusiasm for others is not.

---

[1] *Gautamiya-Tantra / Sanat-Kumar-Samhita*. (The mantra referred to here is the name of Rādhā-Krishna: *gopī-jana-vallabhāya svāha*).
[2] *Bhāgavata Purāṇa* 11.2.34-35

Chapter Four

The Purification Process

You could justifiably ask, "What is the need for a *process* of purification? Why doesn't it happen instantaneously?" After all, I said that divine love creates itself, and is all-powerful like Krishna. So what could block or delay such a self-sufficient all-powerful thing from manifesting?

You are right! There is no need for a process of purification. Divine love *instantly* purifies the soul. That is why authentic *śāstra* makes statements like:

> *As the rising sun instantly destroys the darkness, the holy name* **instantly** *destroys all karmas.*[1]

---

[1] *Nama-kaumudi* 1.2

And:

> *Even the most sinful person can attain liberation the very first time they hear your name.*[1]

And there is the entire amazing story of Ajāmila, for whom even a facsimile of the holy name immediately purified all good and bad *karma.*

Divine love can and should manifest instantaneously and in full perfection. Sometimes it does. But most of the times it doesn't. Why not?

Divine love usually evolves gradually in progressive stages and steps because the vast majority of us are not ready, willing or able to accept her in her full, immediate perfection. It is a lack of receptivity in us, not a lack of power in *bhakti*, which can make devotional enlightenment a long, slow process. The more stubbornly we cling to our familiar self-oriented ego, the longer and slower the process elaborates upon itself. The more readily we embrace our divine Krishna-oriented ego, the quicker and easier the process becomes – to the point of instantaneous perfection being a valid possibility.

---

[1] *Bhāgavata Purāṇa* 6.16.44

What makes us so unreceptive?

Selfishness. A selfless heart is soft and receptive like a sponge – instantly absorbing everything you pour into it. Selfishness, however, creates hard calluses over the heart, which takes time and effort to soften. And so, Bhāgavata says:

> *If you chant the holy name without melting, crying, and getting goose bumps, your heart must be hard like iron.*[1]

Even selfless people can experience a slight delay in getting the perfection of divine love. "Even a healthy tree waits for the right season to bear its fruit."

What is this "right season"? Sometimes it is a timing that allows historically important and instructive events to unfold. For example, Ajāmila was without offense, but he did not become pure until the famous events surrounding his brush with death unfolded.

In most cases, the "right season" is a timing of ripeness. Krishna sometimes delays the fructification of divine love so that the tree first

---

[1] *Bhāgavata Purāṇa* 2.3.24

reaches the absolute height of strength, thus delivering the supreme fruit. It is said that he behaved in this way with the Pāṇḍavas - orchestrating apparently karmic distresses in their lives, which intensified their relationship to him and thus made their realization of divine love even more perfect and sweet.

This is why he says:

> *When I wish to be very merciful to someone I take away everything they have until they have nothing at all but me.*[1]

Divine love *can* appear instantly in her full glory but usually there is some delay. In some cases this delay is an intentional divine plan, but in most cases it occurs because our hearts only gradually become willing to let go of selfish impurities. Thus the vast majority of practitioners go through *stages* of purification.

Stages of Purification

[1] *Bhāgavata Purāṇa* 10.88.8

Although any devotional practice will purify us, we should concentrate primarily on *nāma-saṁkīrtana.* Devotional practices are like food; they nourish the heart of the soul. Yet, when I am very ill, I have no appetite. Very ill people need *medicine:* food with super-concentrated nutritional value - so they can gain nourishment even by eating only the very little their weak appetite will allow. Similarly, we should concentrate only on the most powerful devotional practice: dancing and singing the divine names of Krishna, *nāma-saṁkīrtana.* Gradually but effectively this will restore health to the soul, reviving her appetite for pure devotion.

Our receptivity to the blessings of divine love is proportionate to our appetite for it. The wise say that this appetite returns in nine distinct stages, as we have been discussing. The first stage was to gain *conviction* in the value of divine love. The second stage was to seek *guidance* towards divine love. The third stage was to put that guidance into *practice.* The fourth stage, purification, began as a result of that practice. During this fourth stage, the soul is cured from the vast majority of selfishness.

Different infections cure at different rates, because each has a different resistance to the medicine of devotional practice. The four branches of infection, as mentioned earlier, are:

1. The desire to enjoy good karma

2. The desire to not suffer bad karma

3. The desire to be popular and powerful in a "spiritual" context

4. Disinterest in devotion, in preference for selfish emotions like envy, hatred, anger, etc.

The first two infections - desires to enjoy and not suffer - have the least resistance. Relatively quickly, they disappear almost entirely. The third infection - exploiting devotion for selfish rewards like fame and power - is more resistant at first, but once it goes, it goes quickly and completely. The fourth infection is by far the most virulent and resistant even to concentrated and prolonged treatment. This persistent virus remains clinging on to our hearts right up until the very end of our illness.

To explain the above in more detail, impurities disappear in five distinct stages:

1.	**Singly**	Only one or two selfish traits disappear.
2.	**Plurally**	Entire groups of selfish traits have disappeared.
3.	**Mostly**	The majority of selfish traits are gone.
4.	**Completely**	All selfish traits are gone.
5.	**Irrevocably**	Selfish traits can never return.

The following graph shows the rates at which the four infections of selfishness tend to cure. It groups together the first two infections, attachment to enjoyment and aversion to suffering, because they are two sides of the same coin, and cure at the same speed. The graph labels this category as "karma." The third infection, trying to enjoy within the context of devotional service, is labeled "*bhakti.*" The fourth infection, being indifferent and hostile towards selfless devotion, is labeled "offense."

The vertical axis represents the percentage of purification. *Singly*= 25%. *Plurally* = 50%. *Mostly* = 75%. *Completely* = 95%. *Irrevocably* = 100%. The horizontal axis represents the nine stages of evolution towards divine love, *prema.*

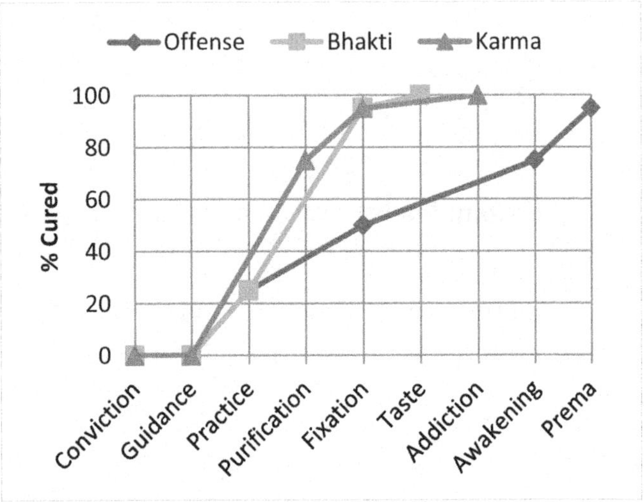

Selfishness related to material enjoyment and suffering loses hold over *most* of my heart at the fourth stage, *purification.* At the fifth stage, *fixedness*, it *completely* disappears. At the seventh stage, *addiction*, it is *irrevocably* destroyed.

Selfishness exploiting the guise of devotion only *singly* relents during the third stage, *practice.* By the fifth stage, *fixedness*, I have *completely* given this up. At the sixth, *taste*, it is *irrevocably* gone forever.

Selfishness manifesting as disinterest in and neglect for devotion relents only *singly* during *practice*. By the fifth stage, *fixedness*, it disappears *plurally*. Not until the eighth stage, *awakening*, are these impurities *mostly* cured! By the ninth and final stage, *prema*, they are *completely* cured, but it is not until I actually become directly involved in Krishna's pastimes that are gone forever, *irrevocably*.

Impossibility of Relapse

A question arises: "If the final impurities are irrevocably destroyed by attaining the loving association of Krishna, why do some persons in direct association with Krishna appear to have committed offenses?"

Two historical examples are: 1. King Citraketu, and 2. Jaya and Vijaya. King Citraketu had attained *prema* but still seemed to offend Śiva and thus suffer the curse of his wife, Pārvatī. Similarly, Jaya and Vijaya, Nārāyaṇa's gatekeepers, seemed to offend the Four Kumāra and thus suffer their curse to become history's most powerful opponents of Viṣṇu. However, these are *not* true offenses because neither Citraketu nor Jaya and Vijaya had any selfishness in their hearts at all.

Citraketu wanted to help people who cheapened and imitated Śiva's behavior, so he involved himself in a sequence of events that demonstrated the caliber of Śiva's purity - humbly, at his own expense. Jaya and Vijaya wanted Nārāyaṇa to enjoy a good fight with a worthy opponent. Their subsequent "insults" to the Four Kumāra were just a drama to fulfill this devotional desire, again at their own apparent expense. [1]

---

[1] Citraketu was enlightened by the words of Nārada on the occasion of his dear son's death. He then began the path of *bhakti*. In his next life he became a heavenly musician and attained *prema* and the direct audience of Saṅkarṣan-Krishna. Later, he attended a dissertation given by Śiva. While teaching, Śiva kept his lovely wife seated on his lap. Citraketu criticized this, thinking it a bad example. Śiva smiled but his wife became very upset and cursed Chitraketu to be born as a demon. As the demon, Vṛtrāsura, *prema* was never absent from his heart. When Indra came to kill Vṛtrāsura with a thunderbolt, beautiful prayers of pure love for Krishna poured forth. Indra killed him and he attained his rightful position again in the transcendental realm, situated in divine love.

Jaya and Vijaya were great warriors, guardians of the gates into the spiritual world. They thought, "Everyone wants to please Nārāyaṇa by serving him, but Nārāyaṇa also likes to wrestle! We can't really do that here, it would spoil the reverent mood. So we should become his enemies in the material world so we can please him like this." Just then, the four child-sages came to the gate. Jaya and Vijaya insulted them by denying them entry. The children cursed the gatekeepers to become demons for three births - satisfying their spiritual desire to serve Nārāyaṇa.

Therefore even in these very rare and extreme examples we see that once attaining Krishna's direct association in divine love, it is not possible to devalue divine love and become selfish and offensive.

Chapter Five

Fixedness[1]

As we become pure, our practice becomes more deep, sincere, attentive, and steady. In a word, we attain *fixedness* in our practice. The *Bhāgavata* describes the progression from *practice* through *purification* to *fixedness:*

> *Discussing and celebrating Krishna in a humble, loving mood is the best activity. It impels Krishna to purify his dwelling place, your heart.*
>
> *As your heart becomes more pure, you will discuss and celebrate Krishna ever more attentively and fixedly.*

---

[1] *Niṣṭhā*

Thus you will rise above the effects of passion and lethargy to attain the steady and peaceful situation of clarity.[1]

Kīrtan, the main practice of divine love, purifies the heart - liberating it from the ropes of nature's lower modes – ignorance and passion – allowing the higher mode, clarity, to shine more steadily. Thus our practice gradually becomes *fixed* - freed from the sloth of lethargy or the distractions of passion.

The sloth and distraction of nature's lower modes present five specific obstacles to *fixed* devotional practice:

1. ***Drowsiness***	I literally fall asleep during devotional practices.
2. ***Distraction***	If not sleeping, I am distracted by self-centered thoughts.
3. ***Disinterest***	The root of drowsiness and distraction is disinterest: lack of any specific, compelling *interest* in loving Krishna.

[1] *Bhāgavata Purāṇa* 1.2.17-19. One salient point well worth noting is that the *Bhāgavata Purāṇa* here defines *kīrtan* and *kathā* ("celebration" and "discussion" of Krishna) as the sum and substance of all practices of divine love.

4. *Deep desires*	The root of disinterest is too much interest in selfish ambitions and prestige and self-defense.
5. *(No) enjoyment*	The root of selfish desire is my habituation to selfish enjoyment instead of the selfless enjoyment of divine love.

Attaining Fixedness

Devotional practices can be physical, verbal, and mental. An example of physical practice is *nāma-saṁkīrtan* - because it involves dancing and playing musical instruments. Examples of verbal practice are *nāma-japa* - chanting without music and dancing, and *bhāgavata-śravaṇa* - discussing Krishna. An example of mental practice is serving Krishna in meditation.

These three types of practice mature to *fixation* at different rates. Physical practice overcomes the five obstacles the most rapidly. It is relatively easy to avoid sleepiness, for example, when dancing or playing a drum and singing Krishna's beloved name among other devotees in *nāma-saṁkīrtan*. It is less easy to avoid sleepiness when listening to someone speak about Krishna, and even more difficult during meditation.

Therefore *fixation* usually first comes to our physical practices, before showing up in our verbal practices and, last of all, solidifies our mental practices. There can be exceptions to this principle. Some people, for example, are naturally better suited for mental practices, so some may attain fixation in that type of practice first.

The Measure of Advancement

As we become fixed in devotional practice, we develop purity and good character traits like humility, respect, friendliness, and compassion. Some people already have many such qualities before even practicing divine love. So you can't really evaluate your advancement in devotion on the basis of these qualities alone. The only true criteria for evaluating one's advancement is this: "As much as I deeply, sincerely, and consistently concentrate on my devotional practice – to that extent I have attained *fixation*, the fifth level of advancement." There is no other reliable measure of success.

Chapter Six

Taste[1]

In a goldsmith's forge, raw ore is placed into the fire, where it remains cold and solid for a while but soon begins to melt and give off a beautiful golden glow. Your heart is such a forge, divine love is the gold, and your devotional practices are the fire. After practicing for some time, the gold in your heart will begin to glow beautifully.

The golden luster of divine love is very attractive and delightful. So, when it began to shine in my heart I immediately developed natural and spontaneous attraction to it. I got a "taste" for my practices.

To get gold to melt, you have to apply steady and intense heat. Similarly, to really experience

---

[1] *Ruci*

the beauty of divine love, I had to practice steadily and intensely. This is why *taste* comes after *fixedness.*

The *Bhāgavata* gives an example of someone attaining *taste* for his or her devotional practices:

> *The saint Nārada said, "When I fixed my mind steadily upon my devotional practices I gained an extremely pleasant and purifying taste for them."*[1]

Another example: Studies initially feel tedious and hairsplitting because the student doesn't yet really comprehend the significance of what she is studying. But as she begins to "get it" the subject that was once dreadfully hard gradually becomes genuinely interesting and rewarding.

Another example: A man with jaundice eats rock candy as part of the ayurvedic cure. At first his disease makes the sugar taste as bitter as chewing aspirin. If he can stick to a regular regimen, however, he will regain normal health bit-by-bit, day-by-day, and sweetness will return to the taste of sugar.

---

[1] *Bhāgavata Purāṇa* 1.5.27

All these examples illustrate that we must stick steadily to a fixed regimen of devotional practices - despite our lack of natural interest in them. Doing so allows them to purify our heart, allowing us to appreciate the luster of pure love and thus develop true, honest, and natural attraction to our devotional practices. Before we attain *taste*, we have to make strenuous efforts to concentrate deeply upon our practices, but once we develop taste for them we will effortlessly concentrate without distraction.

The *Bhāgavata* describes the effortless fixation that comes from *taste*:

> *Nārada said, "Discussion of their sweetheart Krishna flows from their mouths like a river flooding in all directions! Those who drink from this river never tire of it, and are not distracted at all by ordinary hungers, thirsts, fears, etc."*[1]

Stages of Taste

---

[1] *Bhāgavata Purāṇa* 4.29.40

There are two stages of *taste:* 1. taste that is dependent on external qualities, and 2. taste that is not.

It is like this: A starving man enjoys any food at all, but a person with a weak appetite is picky. Similarly, when my appetite for devotion is only just beginning to awaken I will only enjoy devotional practices that are very expertly performed, but when that appetite is more fully bloomed it creates a hunger that allows me to relish *any* devotional practice, no matter how poor the external appearance of it.

At first I experienced the sweet taste of *nāma-saṁkīrtan* if it was led by a sweet singer with deep devotion and accompanied by expert and devoted musicians, but now I relish the joy of *kīrtan* from the very first syllable of the first mantra, without waiting to figure out if the singer is good, etc. If the *kīrtan* is well done, however, my joy knows no bounds!

At first I enjoyed hearing about Krishna if the speaker was learned, deep, dramatic, poetic, etc., but now I relish the topic regardless of the qualification or expertise of the speaker. If the speaker is good, I relish it even more deeply.

At first I enjoyed seeing the deities of Krishna when they were specially dressed and decorated. Now, I always enjoy the opportunity to see Krishna's deity, and if there is nice paraphernalia my joy floods beyond limit!

Diary of the Hungry

"Oh, Friend, why are you disregarding the delicious name of Krishna and giving all your attention to earning money? Do you enjoy it? I think it will only make you tired and worried!"

I blurted this out spontaneously, but then felt bad - becoming aware of my own similar faults. So I continued: "I'm sorry I am so shameless. Who am I to talk like this? I criticize you but I am in a far worse position! Just look at me, I got the precious seed of divine love from my dear guru but what did I do with it? I just tied it up in a cloth and hid it deep in my pockets. Forgetting that I have a gem in my pocket, I run around chasing costume jewelry: unreal and fleeting pleasures in a material masquerade dimly resembling life.

"But that's just me: a weakling addicted to licking bitter things like gossip and criticism and pretending they are sweet - meanwhile ignoring delicious things like Krishna's names, qualities, and pastimes - thinking that they are bitter. If you start talking about Krishna I nod off to sleep, but if you whisper some gossip about your neighbor's daughter my ears snap to attention like soldiers! I dress like a spiritualist, but underneath I am a stain on the cloth of spiritualism. I am getting old, but still act like a teenager irresponsibly chasing any opportunity to gratify my genitals, satisfy my stomach, or widen my wallet."

I then hurry to find a book about Krishna and start reading it eagerly, drinking it like a bee drinking from a flower. Unable to contain myself, I begin discussing the wonders of what I just read. This inevitably carries me into the company of devotees continuously engaged in *nāma-kīrtana* and discussions of Krishna's pastimes, beauty, and delightful qualities. Eventually it brings me to the root of such assemblies, the holy land of Vṛndāvana where I totally lose myself to all the different devotional activities overflowing there.

People look at me strangely. I am odd and distracted, because my mind is always on Krishna. The taste I enjoy in my devotional practices is like my dance instructor. From her I learn my very first lessons on how to dance in *kṛṣṇa-līlā*.

Learning this dance is more delightful than anything I have ever experienced. Soon, my teacher will bring me to her own instructors, *bhāva* and *prema,* for more advanced lessons in the delicious dance of divine ecstasy.

Chapter Seven

Addiction[1]

We typically think of "addiction" as a negative, debilitating condition, but the truth is that by our very nature we are always addicted to something. Addiction to the wrong things is negative and debilitating, but addiction to the divine beloved precipitates enlightenment.

In *Bhāgavata*, The sage Kapila told his mother:

> *The mind, by its very nature, is always addicted to something. Addiction to material sensations causes bondage, but addiction to the Supreme Personality causes liberation.*[2]

---

[1] *Āsakti*
[2] *Bhāgavata Purāṇa* 3.25.15

Addiction results from taste. One's first "taste" of heroine, for example, soon develops into an addiction to the drug itself. Similarly, first I got a deep taste for devotional practice, and this soon developed into an addiction to the focal point of those practices: Krishna. Initially, a drug user is fascinated by the parties and other interesting things that accompany drug culture, but when truly addicted all she can think about is her need for the drug itself. In just this way, I was at first fascinated by the taste of devotional practices but now I am addicted to the "drug itself," the actual source of all that exciting taste: Rasarāja Krishna, the Monarch of Flavor.

At first, the drug user has other things in his life besides the drug, but eventually a true addict becomes oblivious to all other concerns; Nothing matters except the drug. This is how it works in divine love, too. At first my taste for devotional practice shared my attention with my taste for other things. Now, however, at the stage of addiction I am absolutely oblivious to everything except my divine beloved, unaware that other things like pain and pleasure or honor and dishonor even exist. I am now completely shameless in my dire pursuit of divine love.

Bhāgavata describes this:

> *Enjoying the taste of Krishna makes one absolutely shameless and outright addicted to singing his names and stories without a care in the world for what anyone thinks of it.*[1]

I used to make strenuous efforts to continuously drag me back to my devotional practices. It seemed like a hopeless, endless task. But as I began to develop *taste* it became very easy to fix my heart and mind on my delightful practices, for long stretches of time, and to great depths of concentration. Now that I am becoming *addicted*, my heart and mind are so tightly wrapped around their hopes to taste Krishna, it is almost impossibly laborious to drag them *away* from devotional practice!

When I used to try to focus on Krishna, I couldn't really figure out how and when my attention would wind up somewhere else. Now, as I try to go about normal daily life I am at a loss to explain how and when my attention winds up again completely enrapt in Krishna.

Flower Buds on the Vine of Divine Love

---

[1] *Bhāgavata Purāṇa* 11.2.39

At the stage of *addiction*, delicate green flower buds appear on the vine of divine love. When you see a bud on a plant you know there will soon be a flower. Similarly, when I attain *addiction* to Krishna I know that the flower of spiritual awakening *(bhāva)* is coming within my hopeful reach. I am getting much closer to actually realizing divine love! I am getting close to actually *meeting* Krishna!!! I begin to catch fleeting glimpses of momentary visions of Krishna within my heart.

In the *Bhāgavata*, Nārada describes the momentary vision of Krishna that he had at the stage of *addiction:*

> *When Krishna heard me sing about him with the voice of addiction he momentarily appeared in my heart, as if beckoned by my singing.*[1]

Diary of an Addict

One morning I saw a devotee. "Hello there!" I called. "What's that necklace? It has a beautiful locket - is your Śālagrāma Śila inside!? I see your

---

[1] *Bhāgavata Purāṇa* 1.6.34

mouth moving slightly as you walk. You must be relishing the delicious taste of Krishna's name! Just seeing you makes me feel happy and fortunate! Talk to me! Tell me about the holy places you have visited, the great souls you've met, and the realizations they have blessed you with! What a perfect life you have! I want to become more like you, so please talk to me about all this!!!"

Later on, wandering about, I encountered another devotee. "What is that beautiful book you have under your arm? I bet it is the Tenth Canto of *Śrīmad Bhāgavatam*! You must be studying it? Please, just for a moment or two, share with me something you have learned! Won't you please at least recite one verse for me? My ears are parched, and your words would be like the sweetest water!"

Soon I again found myself wandering, hunting for more opportunities like these. Immense fortune fell to me for some unknown reason, and I chanced upon a larger gathering of devotees - surely they could easily destroy all my misery and loneliness! I bowed eagerly to the group and they welcomed me affectionately. Their leader called me to sit near him. I embarrassed myself, being unable to hold back my tears as I said, "You are the best doctor in the world because you can cure the worst disease, which infects every single living thing in this universe. I am so sick! Please take my pulse, diagnose me and give me a prescription to make me well!"

That great, exalted soul then instructed me in the proper practice of Hari Bhajan - devotional service. Overjoyed, I could not leave his side for almost a week! I remained there to serve him and practice under his guidance.

I don't really recall how, when, or why, but I again found myself wandering around looking for more devotional nectar. I was in a small forest and saw a deer. Krishna is beautiful like deer, so I thought, "If the deer comes towards me it means that Krishna will be merciful to me, but if the deer runs away I am doomed."

It ran away, and I fell into a depression. At the edge of the trees I chanced upon four young, carefree *brāhmaṇa* children playing. Who knows, maybe they were the Four Kumāra? So I inquired humbly, "Dear children, will I ever get the chance to see the Son of Nanda?"

They said "No," and went on playing.

Why??? Sadly, I wandered back home where pale anxieties covered my face. What if the deer and children are right??? Where can I find Krishna!? When? How?

Perturbed and constantly distracted, I sometimes managed a few winks of sleep before I suddenly snaped awake in the middle of the night, plagued by fear that I may not ever see him. My family tried to help, but what could they really do? I could barely even *hear* their words. They just thought I was going crazy, and they seemed to be right. I didn't know how to explain what I was going through, so mostly I just sat silently.

The neighbors said, "They were always a strange family." Priests thought I was a fool and a nuisance. Philosophers thought I was a sentimentalist. Moralists condemned me for the trouble I was inadvertently putting my poor family through. Even most devotees thought I was just trying to put on a show to impress people. But one or two among them were my only safe haven in the world. Only they understood me. Still, even they did not understand the pain I was in. They thought I attained the greatest thing, but actually I was just on the edge of it, and felt its absence so very painfully.

Chapter Eight

Awakening[1]

Addiction to Krishna becomes a fever more dire by the day, drying out the ego surrounding my soul. This allows sparks of divine energy (which have always been all around me) to reignite my being, casting light on my inherent nature of eternality, awareness and bliss. Meanwhile, my false ego burns to ash, and the darkening modes of nature can no longer hide the brilliant effulgence of my latent spiritual identity. My true being, as a divine lover of Krishna, awakens.

Now the flower-buds on the wish-fulfilling vine of divine love blossom! Even the outside of their fresh petals is impossibly beautiful, because the seductive allure of truly blossoming divine love is

---

[1] *Bhāva*

nearly impossible to even comprehend.[1] The inner whorl of this new flower wreaks utter ruin on all other things of beauty, even the beauty of spiritual liberation.[2]

Wholly and Irresistibly Drawn to Krishna

The child-saint Prahlād described what devotion is like at this stage:

> *Little pieces of iron automatically fly to a big magnet. That is how my emotions feel when Viṣṇu comes into my mind. They automatically and helplessly fly towards him.*[3]

My five senses, mind, intellect, and ego are helplessly pulled towards Krishna like iron filings towards a huge magnet.

And he is drawn to me! The awakening of divine love liquefies all my emotions, and turns them into a magical perfume emanating from the flower of my heart. This intoxicating aroma

---

[1] *Sudūrlabhā* - the impossible rarity of the treasure of divine love.
[2] *Moksha-laghuta-krit* - divine love makes even enlightenment and liberation seem like trivialities.
[3] *Bhāgavata Purāṇa* 7.5.14

spreads luxuriantly through all time and space, and enters the nostrils of bee-like Krishna, seducing his attention and enchanting him to come closer and closer to me in person. Its fragrance is so powerful that it causes the Supreme Being to be drawn to a tiny entity such as I, like a bumble bee to a spring flower!

Maybe that's why I sometimes notice the creator of this universe, Brahmā Jī, bowing down to me at a respectful distance? Whatever. I have no time to think about that. All I can think about is the fact that Krishna must be seeking the source of the new fragrance of love that has seduced his fancy. *Any second now* I will see him face to face! All my senses burn in an inferno of expectant yearning:

The crimson glow
of his lips, and the rims of his eyes

The white effulgence
of the gentle smile on his moonlike face

The golden luster
of his stylish clothes and jewelry

Expecting to see such sights
At any moment
My eyes have drenched my entire body in tears

The distant notes
of a melodious flute

The rhythmic chimes
of graceful ankle bells

The sonorous words
of a mesmerizing voice, beckoning me

Yearning for these sounds
To dance as even the faintest echo
My ears are snapped to attention at all times

A dark but brilliant lily
Mimics, but dimly
The graceful, soothing touch of his hand

The hairs on my skin stand up
Stretching to be even a few millimeters closer
To that ever-expected touch

Why do my nostrils flare so wide?
Why do I breathe so long and deep?

Like a deer, I search
For a trace
Of his intoxicating, divine fragrance.

Why do I always lick my lips?
Day-dreaming
Afraid to even ask the question
That steals my mind:

Will I ever taste, firsthand
the nectar of his lips???

All I can accomplish, however,
Is a long, deep, pitiful sigh...

In my mind's eye I sometimes actually *see* Krishna. It is so intense that I mistake it for reality and plunge into an incomparably sweet intoxication. But when the vision subsides and I know it was just a "dream" I sink into the lowest depression.

My intellect can make no plan other than trying to figure out how my senses can experience

Krishna. Awake, dreaming, or even in the deepest sleep I can't stop trying to figure out how to do it!

"I am his." This concept has stolen my ego. "Me" used to be a word that referred to my body, but now I am barely even aware if I still wear such a costume. The shape and form of my spiritual self has awakened and become *me*. "He is mine!" He is the only thing I want to possess. Like a hungry man about to be given a sumptuous feast, I am eager and greedy to take possession of Krishna and thereby relish the right to lovingly serve him at all times!

Symptoms of *Bhāva*

It is not easy to spot people who have attained the eighth stage, *bhāva.* For one thing, they are *exceedingly* rare. Another complication is the fact that *bhāva* makes a person behave strangely and want to hide their achievement.

Why do they hide themselves? If you had a winning lottery ticket, you would get strange. You would be so protective of the ticket - afraid of having it stolen or lost - that you would irrationally hide it until you could actually claim the prize. *Bhāva* is a lot like a winning lottery ticket because one still needs to claim the prize - *prema.* Someone who attains this level behaves strangely, compulsively trying to protect what he has attained by hiding it.

Considering this, how can we spot a person on the eighth level of advancement?

Some people think *bhāva* is evident by the display of extremely powerful emotions or ecstatic symptoms: getting goose bumps when hearing about Krishna; crying profusely and uncontrollably while dancing and singing Krishna's names; stuttering and becoming choked up when trying to talk about Krishna. But these emotional displays do not conclusively demonstrate the attainment of *bhāva,* because they could result from other things:

- I might be in the physical or emotional proximity of more advanced souls who have attained *bhāva,* and the depth of their emotion simply reflects off me temporarily.

- I might have ordinary material emotions, and the name, form, etc. of Krishna might simply remind me of these.

- I might just be a very good *actor*, intentionally imitating devotional symptoms for some relatively nefarious reason.

It is only by one's character that the attainment of the eighth stage can surely be known. *Bhāva* unfailingly generates eight telltale character traits:[1]

1. Not being bothered even when things are bothersome
2. Valuing each moment spent in Krishna's service
3. Lack of interest in sense objects
4. Feeling humble and grateful in spite of being most exalted and deserving
5. Absolutely knowing that you can accomplish the "impossible" and attain Krishna directly
6. Extreme enthusiasm to do so
7. Constant enjoyment of Krishna's name, form, activities, etc.
8. Tender devotion for the places Krishna lives, like Vṛṇdāvana

---

[1] *Bhakti Rasamrita Sindhu* 1.3.25-26

A person who has attained *bhāva* will try to hide emotional displays, but they cannot hide these eight character traits.

Two Schools of *Bhāva*

Inner spiritual awakening *(bhāva)* arises from addiction to devotional practices *(āsakti)*. However, the two schools of devotional practice produce different degrees of awakening. One school *(vaidhi)* practices devotion because it is right and proper to love God. The other *(rāgānugā)* practices devotion out of an emotional interest in doing so. Both schools of practice can generate spiritual awakening, but the degree of awakening resulting from emotional compulsion is more profound and profuse. It is so strong and abundant that it even overwhelms Godhead, eclipsing his majestic and official status and inviting him into truly intimate personal relationships that would not otherwise be plausible to have with a figure as imposing as the Supreme Being.

Five Flavors of Love

Water falls on the ground and energizes different plants. The water is identical but the different plants produce different fruits: one a mango, another a jackfruit, another sugarcane, while yet another makes grapes. All the fruits are sweet and delicious, but jackfruits are sweeter than mango, sugarcane sweeter than jackfruit, and grapes the sweetest of all.

This is a metaphor where *bhāva* is the water. The different plants are different individuals. The same spiritual energy *(bhāva)* flowers differently in different people. In all cases the flower eventually produces a sweet fruit, but the flavor of each is unique. There are five broad categories of flavor:

1. Appreciation
2. Service
3. Friendship
4. Protection
5. Romance

Just as grapes are sweeter than mangoes, romantic emotions are sweeter than those that are merely appreciative. This is not a subjective statement. It is an objective truth because each succeeding variety of emotion builds upon the emotions that preceeds it. Thus the sweetness of the former flavor of divine emotion also exists within the later, yet the same is not true in reverse. In servitude, for example, there is also appreciation for the beloved. But in appreciation alone there is no active service. In friendship there is also service, but in servitude there is no friendship as a peer. Romantic emotion is the "sweetest" or "best" of the emotions that a heart can produce because it includes all the other types of emotion: appreciation of Krishna, desire to be useful to Krishna, friendship and camaraderie with Krishna, and protectiveness of Krishna, yet romantic emotion is the only one with full, unregulated intimacy in all respects.

Even though grapes are sweeter than mangoes many people just *like* mangoes better than they like grapes. This *is* a subjective statement. Similarly, each individual has a latent spontaneous preference for a particular flavor of affection for Krishna. That is the flavor that blooms in their heart when they reach the stage of awakening. That is the flavor that is "the best" *for them.*

The specific flavor of spiritual love that awakens in me is the foundation upon which I will soon experience the full ecstasy of divine love.

This foundation *(sthayi-bhava)* needs appropriate stimuli *(vibhava)*. Then it bursts into action through voluntary expressions *(anu-bhava)* and involuntary reactions *(sattvika-bhava)*, creating emotional waves *(vyabhichari-bhava)* that raise the ocean of ecstasy.

The ecstasy of divine love *(rasa)* results from the interplay of these five factors. It does not really happen until I reach the ninth stage, *prema*, because it is not until then that I will really meet the essential stimulus: the Son of Nanda, Sri Krishna.

Other forms of Godhead can also stimulate divine *rasa* in the hearts of their devotees, to some extent, since they are expansions of Krishna. After all, rivers and streams do contain some water, though they are not the ocean. However, Nanda's son, Krishna, is the original ocean of all *rasa*. He alone most perfectly and absolutely fulfills the *Upanishadic* definition of the Absolute: "He is *Rasa*. Attaining him one becomes limitlessly blissful." He alone is the most perfect stimulus for divine ecstasy.

Chapter Nine

Divine Love[1]

The flowering vine of devotion now sprouts many new shiny, smooth, beautiful leaves. Like the first two leaves she sprouted, these are composed of devotional "practices" like hearing and chanting. But they are so much more smooth and beautiful than the first leaves because they are not activities to *attain* love; they are activities which *express* love.

Every part of the vine that has developed since it first peeked out from the soil of my heart now shines with unlimited health and beauty! The "older" parts of the vine become brand new because the same things I once did to *search* for devotion I now do to *express* devotion. Expressing my devotion to Krishna in these ways inspires the flower of my *bhāva* to transform into a fruit: *prema.*

Lifetime after lifetime, I followed thousands of selfish desires like a lost soul trying to find his way home in the dark night by following the

---

[1] *Prema*

twinkling stars. When I began my spiritual quest I set off in a different direction, trying to ignore these selfish desires. Eventually I was able to forego and forget them, but now that the brilliant sun of divine love has risen in the sky of my heart, I can no longer see those stars, even if I tried.

Once upon a time thousands of emotional ropes tied me to my body, family, house, money, etc. But now divine love effortlessly unties these knots, spiritualizes my emotional "ropes," and fastens them to Krishna's sweet name, form, qualities, and pastimes.

The vine of divine love has borne fruit. The taste of that fruit is *condensed, unique bliss.*[1] The fresh deliciousness of this fruit has the power to attract even the All-Attractive, Krishna.[2]

The Edge of Divine Madness

By tasting the unique bliss condensed in the fruit of divine love, I have plunged into the wildest intoxication. Heedless of all restrictions and

---

[1] *sandrānanda-viśeṣātmā*
[2] *śrī-kṛṣṇa-karṣinī*

obstacles, I become oblivious to concepts like *proper* and *improper*. I smash and stumble and thrash my way through all such meaningless things like a person set aflame would recklessly sprint towards a pool. Burning with millions of maddening desires to meet Krishna, I bolt towards the cool, moonlit lake of even a momentary vision of him.

When I leap into these ponds, the heat of my mad desires vaporizes their waters and refuses to abate. Visions of Krishna may look like a cool lake, but it acts like gasoline, strengthening the flames of my need to *really* have Krishna. Soon I am caught in an inferno of such staggering proportions that my body itself feels like it is about to vaporize.

Is this a house I live in, or is it a bramble of thorns in a haunted forest? The people in this house - are they my relatives or are they dangerous wells overgrown with serrated grasses? I sit here to eat a meal, but is it nourishment or punishment?

People sometimes come before me - respected people - and say kind and flattering things to me. The sound of their voice is a snake whose poisoned fangs bite my ears! Then friends appear to console me. Their words feel like acid poured on a wound.

Oh God, I cannot bear this any longer... day after day of the same mundane, boring routines: brushing teeth, showering, cleaning, trying to work... these chores are like nooses in the hands of death!

Then I chance to come before a mirror. What is this ugly thing I see? Each limb is so heavy, difficult to move, and odorous.

Sleep? Perhaps sleep would be better, since being awake is like drowning in a sea of depression! Yes, I wish to sleep and never again awake, but I always wake up - like returning to hell after being allowed to leave for a moment. I awake and lie still. Breath moves in and out of my lungs like winds rustling forgotten husks in a long abandoned farmhouse.

What more can I say to you? Everything that should bring happiness to a normal person is an episode of torture for me. Not even the practices of devotion bring me any relief, for if I start to hear Krishna's name, my very soul feels like it will shatter into a billion shards!

Ah, but the secret is this: The utter madness of my infinite longing for him is an enormous magnet. Krishna is but a tiny iron filing, being helplessly drawn to me.

Divine Perception

I want to describe what it was like to meet Krishna, though of course it is impossible to do so properly. First I want to explain that the Supreme Being is beyond perception, but being beyond limitation he is also beyond imperception. Because of my pure love for him, he sent his own powers of unlimited perception to reside within my senses so that I could *truly* perceive the infinite seductiveness of his form, the transfixion of his fragrance, the bewitching melodies of his voice, and the tender velvet of his touch.

Perceiving Krishna is an experience that only makes you want to perceive *more* of him. This is another thrilling aspect of the *limitlessness* within the "limits" of divine perception. Krishna is an experience that never fades, and constantly intensifies. The more you experience Krishna firsthand, the more you want to experience him. This forms an emotional "feedback loop" that I really shouldn't belittle by comparing it to any ordinary experience. Still, I have to try to convey something to you. Imagine yourself stranded in the middle of a desert, dying of thirst and baked by the relentless sun, with nothing but scorching sand on every horizon. Next, imagine yourself in the cooling shade of a huge banyan's thick, moist leaves, on the bank of the rushing Ganges river with hundreds of clean pitchers of crystal clear, cold water all around you. The feeling of wanting Krishna is like being in the desert. The feeling of having Krishna is like being on the bank of the river. Try to imagine teleporting back and forth from one extreme to another so quickly that you are in both conditions at the same time. That might give you some idea of what it feels like to finally meet Krishna.

Meeting Krishna for the First Time

Now I'll tell you about the first time I met Krishna, and how I attained a transcendental mind and senses as a result.

The first thing I got was the sight of him... his soul-ravishing beauty. The allure of this vision could not be contained in my eyes alone. All my senses melded synestheticly; every sense became visual to see him. My mind couldn't process so much delight, so I fell unconscious.

Krishna sent towards me a breeze carrying the sweet aroma of his divine fragrance. This scent entered my nose and aroused me from my swoon. Yet all my other senses, in a clamor of unprecedented greed, began tripping over one another to for the experience. Another synesthesia allowed every atom of my perceptive being to become transfixed by his fragrance. Under an overload of sensual bliss, again I lost consciousness.

The next thing I remember was his voice, sonorous and melodious. "My love, I am all yours!" He said. "Don't be lightheaded. Take your time. Enjoy me to your heart's content!" The meaning of these words escaped me at the time, the sound alone was so intoxicating and delightful that my senses once again wrapped around themselves and all became like ears to enjoy his delightful voice. In the overload of ecstasy I again swooned.

When I next opened my eyes I was in his arms! He was embracing me to his chest, which was wet with the tears of his joy at meeting me![1] The sensation of divine touch unified all my sensual being, overloaded my mind with rapture and sent me again to the brink of passing out.

But this time, before I could faint entirely, he *kissed* me! Yes, the divine mouth of All-Attractive Krishna *kissed* mine!!! What words in any language can describe the sweetness of that taste? The situation that then ensued in my consciousness was catastrophic in the most wondrously delicious way. In the middle of all my senses trying to experience his touch, he kissed me - and all of my senses tried to become *two senses at once*: touch and taste. The extreme overload of transcendental euphoria destroyed me. I lost all hold of my awareness and was gone.

Krishna himself could not immediately bring me back to external awareness. My mind was not yet capable of processing the data from spiritual sense perception. The overload of sensual ecstasy in Krishna continuously shut it down, as it

---

[1] I have heard that others, who are his servants, awaken by the touch of his feet upon their heads; still others, his friends, awaken by him taking them by the hand; his parents awaken by feeling his tender hand wiping the tears of bliss from their cheeks.

reflexively fled to avoid self-destruction in a melt-down.

Then, out of fathomless magnanimity, Krishna sent into my mind his own powers of limitless spiritual perception so that I could effortlessly comprehend the overwhelming synesthetic experience of Absolute Sweetness simultaneously from all five senses at once! When Krishna's magnanimous potency entered my mind, it commanded my love for him to multiply by infinite factors, setting off a devastating cataclysmic tempest. Thousands of tidal waves, hurricanes and lightning bolts together crashed in perfect synchronicity, annihilating my mind and its ever-limited and ever-imperfect faculty of perception. After this destruction, Krishna's energy commanded my divine love to build a new mind with limitless conduits of infinite interconnection. Thus by his kind compassion I came to possess a limitless mind fit to perceive him in totality.

This new mind processes absolute synesthesia with a flawless efficacy that clarifies and heightens the ability of each individual sense. It is nearly impossible to explain adequately, because there is simply no other experience like it in the least. I can hear, for example, the details of a single flutter in a note from his flute with unparalleled clarity. Yet simultaneously I remain in full awareness of the complete nature of all aspects of the experience of Krishna - visual, aural, olfactory, tactile, and flavor.

In *Bhāgavata*, Kapilā describes this to his mother:

> *When they experience Krishna's playful smile, captivating glance, and enchanting speech, all their senses become completely enrapt in him, and are unable to be aware of anything else. Bhakti then bestows all her fullest blessings, even if they might not personally seek them.*[1]

They say a *cakora* bird only drinks the rain falling from a cloud. My mind is like that: it will only process sensual input coming directly from the monsoon cloudburst of Krishna. Yet my beak always feels too small, wanting passionately to drink every drop of him all at once!

Seeing my lust-like eagerness to relish him, Krishna himself becomes astonished and calls forth his innermost energy - she who sits in the

---

[1] *Bhāgavata Purāṇa* 3.25.26

middle of the lotus of his heart, surrounded by all other divine potencies. Her name is *compassion.*[1] She arises from his heart and wells up in his loving eyes, which glance at me with such romance and charm that my very soul melts. Across the link from his eyes to mine, the warm, sweet energy of compassion enters from him into me and takes command of my ever-melting heart. Enthroned there, she enables my soul to fully relish every drop of Krishna - an experience that makes even liberated souls quiver in astonishment and wonder!

Krishna's compassion is the emperor of all his qualities and the prime minister of all his pastimes. Now that he has sent his compassion to rule the core of my being, I am fit to truly participate in his divine pastimes to the fullest extent. In these sweet pastimes his compassion is so powerful that it allows even the things normally thought of as character flaws to become the most beautiful expressions of divine love. Out of compassion to fulfill the desire of his beloveds, Krishna enjoys being confused, sleepy, intoxicated, jealous, sad, mad, violent, exhausted, hungry, doubtful, egotistical, partial, and dependent! Seeing the

---

[1] See *Krama-Dipika 1.43: vimalotkarshini jnana kriya yogeti shaktayah, prahvi satya tatheshana-anugraha navami smrita.*

Supreme Being accepting these roles out of sheer love for others, my entire being becomes a flood of tears flowing towards Krishna like a rushing river.

"My love!" went the song of his affectionate voice, "It has been such a long time, many lifetimes, that you have been putting yourself through hell for my sake, foregoing the common comforts of a happy, healthy family, disregarding taunts and insults from society and even from your friends. Out of desire to attain me, you reduced yourself to begging, barely scraping up enough money to make ends meet. You tolerated the cold and the wind. You endured hunger and thirst. You took all sorts of pains and faced life-threatening diseases and dangers - just for the sake of serving me! How can I begin to repay priceless love like that?

"I could make you the ruler of the entire earth; I could make you the king of the demigods in heaven; I could give you mastery over all the forces of nature; but none of those things has any value in comparison to the incomparable love you showered upon me for so long. It would be an *insult* to offer you such things - like giving a plate full of straw and hay to an important guest! You have given me your very self. What can I offer you in return except *my* very self?

"My sweet love, I congratulate you. You have conquered God. I have fallen completely in love with you! I am yours."

My ears embraced each word and enthusiastically pinned them on like splendid earrings. Then I said to him, "My sweet husband! Dearest wellspring of good fortune! Beloved ocean of compassion! I fell into a selfish life of illusion like a girl stumbling into a swamp of ferocious crocodiles. You saw me being torn apart in the jaws of suffering and your butter-soft heart melted, unable to bear my pain! Then, through my guru, you beheaded the tormenting crocodiles by sending your razor-sharp discus in the form of knowledge and understanding.

"Then, again through my guru, you whispered into my ear the divine *mantra* that would erase my false ego and transform me into your loving damsel. You spoke to me about your pastimes, sang your name to me, taught me about yourself, and gradually purified and perfected my genuine love for you by giving me the opportunity to be with and serve people who love you dearly. Despite this overwhelming flood of kindness and mercy, I was so stubborn and reluctant and dull, and made it very difficult and troublesome for you to pull me out of the mire of that swamp. Any ordinary person would have given up on me, but not you!

"You are so humble, gentle and sweet! That's why you feel like I've made efforts to come to you, when the truth is you worked so hard to drag me here. You are not in my debt, my love, just the opposite!

"While you were trying to bring me here, I was kicking and screaming in protest. I said and did so many unkind and insensitive things to you and yours! Even till just yesterday I was behaving like that. I tried to say that your beauty was similar to a fresh dark rain cloud appearing on a hot summer day. I compared your hue to a blue lotus and a pure sapphire. I wrote that your face was like the full moon and that your feet were like the fresh new leaves spouting at the dawn of the spring. What are these analogies except outright insults!? A sesame seed can't compare to a golden mountain! A chickpea can't compare to a wish-granting diamond! Would a lion not be insulted to be compared to a jackal? Would Garuda not feel offended if compared to a fly? From the first moment I truly saw you, I knew your loveliness to be a flower vine that the cows of my poems cannot reach with the chomping teeth of their blunt metaphors. I thought I was such a witty and talented poet, and I broadcast my tedious words to the world. You are so soft, generous, and kind that you take no offense at my inept and self-serving 'glorifications.' You have overlooked the mountain of my insulting ego and have made me yours!"

In *Bhāgavata*, the divine incarnation Kapilā has documented such things:

> *When I show myself to them personally, they speak with me and express all their heartfelt hopes.*[1]

After this heartfelt conversation, Krishna led me into the wondrous forest of Vṛṇdāvana. Walking along the edge of the Yamunā River, he introduced me to all his friends, Subāla and the others, as well as all his beloved cows. We sat for a while with them all under the Bhandira banyan-tree that is their favorite spot to rest and play.

---

[1] *Bhāgavata Purāṇa* 3.25.35

Then he took me to Govardhana Hill and onward to his home at Nandīśvara Hill. He introduced me to all of his friends and family there, including all his dear housemaids, his brother Balarāma, and his wonderful father and mother!

Finally he brought me to Yogapitha and I met Śrīmatī Rādhārāṇī enthroned there as the most gloriously beautiful queen, along with her dearest friends like Lalitā and Viśākhā. I also met all their maidens, including the most affectionate and talented Śrī Rūpa Mañjarī!

At each encounter a mesmerizing tidal wave of bliss would grow stronger and higher within me. On meeting these friends and confidants of Śrīmatī Rādhārāṇī I could bear the bliss no longer and once again fell into a swoon.

The Final Quest

It may have been a few minutes or more before my eyes suddenly snapped open and alert, eager to again drink the vision of my sweetheart Krishna's thrice curved form. Impossible moments followed ever more slowly after the next impossible moment, until I could no longer deny that Śyāmasundara was nowhere to be seen. Not being able to drink Krishna, my eyes instead poured out so many tears - drenching my entire body.

Was it just a dream?

No, no. When I wake up from sleep my limbs feel drowsy for a while and my eyes feel fuzzy; but I have none of those symptoms right now...

Was I put under some magic spell?

No, no. Magic spells make one troubled not joyful, and I feel such wonderful joy...

Am I going crazy?

No, no. My mind is focused, alert and working well - better than ever...

Was it just a fantasy?

No, no. What I have just seen and felt is so far beyond the power of my imagination to dream up...

Was it another one of those sudden, temporary revelations of Krishna I have been having from time to time?

No, no. This was much different.

I have to accept the conclusion that I have met Krishna and his associates! The joy of that sweet dream-come-true mixed with the sorrow of having lost it makes me fall to the earth, writhing and rolling about in the dust.

In *Bhāgavata*, the saint Nārada described his similar experience:

> *Experiencing him, the explosion of love I felt was uncontainable, causing me to enjoy a thrill of bliss and peace so excessive that my hair stood on end. Completely submerged in a flood of ecstatic feelings, I lost track of who I was, lost consciousness, and thus lost my association with the Supreme Being!*[1]

Only the hope of again getting the opportunity to associate with Krishna keeps me alive through the coming days, but sometimes I get dejected and almost lose hope. At times like that I lose control of my body and usually wind up injuring myself

---

[1] *Bhāgavata Purāṇa* 1.6.18

by falling or rolling or tumbling into things, blinded by my tears and the divine anguish of love.

The days drag on... and on. Should I stand, or sit? I've lost my mind and sometimes it is obvious, as I run all around shouting like a trumpet. At other times people mistake me for some peaceful sage while I sit in one place forever, calm, composed, and deep in thought. I have become completely "irresponsible" to the duties of my external life, I am not even sure, honestly if I still have an external life. Am I alive or dead? Words always fail me. When I try to express myself only gibberish blurts from my mouth. When I try to cover up my embarrassing heartbreak, more nonsense babbles forth. People say I am possessed.

One day, a dear friend came to me in a calmer moment. I manage to reveal everything and feel so much better. Understanding me deeply, my friend declares, "You are the most fortunate person in the universe! You have met the Supreme Personality of Godhead *face to face!!!*" He supports his evaluation of my fortune by reference to the *Bhāgavata*:

> *When devotional practice bears fruit and you attain divine love, you lose grip on your mind and heart - for they melt completely and*

become liquid. You uncontrollably laugh, cry, roar, sing, and dance like a lunatic - not even aware of the world around you.[1]

Hearing this confirmation brings me some peace, but the cloud of doubt again covers my face. "Tell me why," I ask my friend, "Why can't I see him again?"

Deeply, I ponder what might be the answer to that question. Perhaps I had my divine experience because some extremely self-realized *bhakta* sent a particle of grace my way? Or maybe it happened because, once, perchance, I did something that was in some way similar to *bhakti*? Or maybe, once upon a time, I did something for Krishna and, for just a fraction of a moment, I was really sincere in my desire to please him?? Can it be? Or is it more likely that an associate of Krishna has been needlessly kind to me and brought me into that experience, in spite of my being a microcosmic ocean of failings?

What difference does it make anyway? Regardless of why, I met Krishna once and now I

---

[1] *Bhāgavata Purāṇa* 11.2.40

can't find him again. I had a priceless treasure in the palm of my hand, but it slipped from my grasp.

Why???

Surely there is no doubt why: my offenses to Krishna and his devotees. How can I remedy this offense!? I have to get rid of that offense somehow! But how?! Who will I ask? What will I do? Where can I go? It seems like there is no one, no place, no way within this empty world to alleviate the offensive attitude in my heart that keeps me from seeing Krishna again. I have no shelter anywhere and the entire world seems like an inferno licking at my skin, ready to devour me.

I resolve that I must spend some time in solitude. I have to get away from everyone and everything and figure this out once and for all. So I retire secretly to a very lonely spot. There I call out, "Hey Krishna!!! The lotus of your beautiful face sends forth fragrant streams of nectar. This fragrance makes Vṛndāvana a land of perfume-intoxicated honeybees greedy to find the garland of flowers swaying around your neck! The sound of their hungry buzzing fills all directions. Hey Śyāmasundara!!! This bee wants to meet you *one more time.* Just *once* more! If you do this for me I promise I will never ask for anything again!"

This is when the "blur" began. I could no longer tell day from night, waking from sleeping, laughing from crying. I lost the ability to figure out if I was in my body or not! Sometimes I see Krishna everywhere I look, sometimes I cannot find him anywhere. Sometimes I am laughing, dancing and singing, at other times I am lamenting, writhing, and weeping. Everything is becoming and intense blur. Time itself is blurring.

The beautiful *Bhāgavata* also describes this condition:

> *When you are completely drunk you lose all external awareness. You don't know if someone is undressing you or dressing you. That is what divine love is like. The attainment of one's divine self is so intoxicating that one has no idea if he is dressed or naked, sitting or standing, alive or dead.*[1]

At some point the allotted time came for me to die, but *when* that happened, I could not tell you. I did not notice. I did not care. All I know is this: Krishna finally accepted my eager invitations!

---

[1] *Bhāgavata Purāṇa* 11.13.36

That ocean of sweet kindness appeared before me again just as before, face to face. He led me into his abode and gave me *my own place* among his lovers!

The Final Perfection

I have attained the ultimate imperishable perfection: full realization of divine love. I am immersed in a real, tangible loving relationship with the Supreme, All-Attractive Personality. This is the end of the story as far as this book goes, but is only the beginning of my real story.

Perfection continually increases without boundary. The experienced describe it as having six ascending facets: *sneha, māna, praṇaya, rāga, anurāga, bhāva* and *mahābhāva.* These, however, are a "different story" because this book is all about how a normal person like you or I can *attain* the perfection of divine love. How the perfection of divine love develops eternally once it has been attained is not a subject in the scope of this book. The intensity of the depths and heights of emotional experience at such levels of being cannot be contained within a material body. If you want to know more about these things study the highly esoteric book *Ujjvala Nilamani* by Sri Rupa

Goswāmī, under the guidance of one who has realized divine love to some significant extent.

Chapter Ten

Transformation of Ego

The Sanskrit word for ego is *aham-kara:* "the creator of a sense of self." This sense of self (ego) has three distinct facets:

1. **I** — The core concept of identity.
2. **Me** — Things that express "I" - The name, form, attributes, etc. of my body and mind.
3. **Mine** — Things possessed by "I" - relatives and property.

Ego can exist in any of three contexts:

1. **Illusory**

   "I, me, and mine" is established in a temporary, illusory context.
2. **Enlightened**

   The illusory context of "I, me, and mine" is destroyed by knowledge.

3. **Divine love**

"I, me, and mine" is established in the context of the spiritual reality of Godhead.

These three contexts of ego are progressive and evolutionary. Each later context is an improvement upon the former, containing more joy and less suffering than its predecessor. This is why sages describe divine love as "the crown jewel of evolution."[1]

I will give a little more detail about the ego in the context of divine love.

1. **I** — I am part of *him*. I am *his*.
2. **Me** — The beauty and talents of my body and mind are instruments of *his* pleasure.
3. **Mine** — *He*, and he alone, is mine.

We begin with an ego rooted in illusion. In the midst of this ignorance, somehow we allow our hearts to be touched for a brief moment by a person who carries divine love. This marks the

---

[1] *"Puruṣārtha-cudamaṇī." "Prema-puṁārtho-mahān."*

embryonic beginning of the transformation of ego. A seed is planted in our hearts, a tiny notion that "the pleasure of God is my own best interest." This small, curious muse is the mystical agent of true alchemy, which will eventually transmute our ego from the iron of illusion to the shining, molten gold of divine love.

That transmutation progresses in nine distinct stages.

1. First, the tiny idea had to grow into a ***conviction*** strong enough to significantly fascinate our thoughts. 2. Eventually this fascination draws us into the company of people who are more serious about cultivating divine love, and from them we take ***guidance.*** 3. We gradually take this guidance more seriously, and put it into ***practice.***

In these first three stages the ego is still very firmly intertwined with all manner of material illusions. Transmutation proceeds at an almost imperceptible, atomic level. The "iron ego" still looks solid, but important changes are happening beneath the surface, leading to the next stage.

4. Devotional practice forms new pathways in the heart and mind, destroying the old, ignorantly selfish network, effecting a thorough internal *purification.* 5. This purification allows us to

gradually increase the quantity and quality of our practice and achieve *fixedness*.

In these fourth and fifth stages, very noticeable transformations occur in the ego, as it attains and begins to move beyond the enlightened state.

6. Fixed practices give profound spiritual experiences, and we begin to develop a genuine *taste* for the spiritual joy inherent in practicing divine love. As this happens, our ego is becoming more like gold than iron, and we begin to sincerely conceive of "I, me, and mine" in relation to my beloved Krishna!

7. We soon lose the taste for all other things and become shamelessly *addicted* to Krishna, the beloved object of divine love. By now our illusory ego is reduced to a seldom whispered echo, heard only now and then during rare spiritual lulls.

8. Then, it finally happens. The divine ego fully *awakens*. We wholly embrace a wondrous spiritual name, body, appearance, etc. There is a new "I," a new "me," and everything "mine" is Krishna... Krishna.... Krishna. The fading scent of material ego is difficult to even willingly recall, like a dream difficult to remember as it fades from your mind when you awaken.

9. Eventually that dream is completely lost - forever forgotten, obliterated. The transmutation of ego from the iron of illusion to the molten gold of *divine love* is complete.

Direct Perception of Krishna

The Absolute Supreme Personality of Godhead cannot be directly perceived by the ego still rooted in the contexts of illusion or enlightenment. Only the love-soaked ego is fully *open, willing,* and *receptive* to experiencing the Absolute Reality in full, in *person,* with no lies, distortions, veils, or attenuations.

The more the ego roots in divine love, the more directly and tangibly we can experience the All-Attractive Absolute Person: Śrī Krishna. In the beginning, during the stage of *practice*, we can artificially force a semblance of Krishna's name, form, pastimes, and qualities into our mind. As a result of *purification* we can do so with greater *fixedness.* Then, we begin to lose taste for all other perceptions. We eventually become shamelessly *addicted* to these intoxicating meditations, which become so deep that they seem to leave the mind and enter the heart. There are brief, precious instants of seemingly direct perceptions of Krishna.

When the divine-love-ego begins to *awaken,* the deepest meditational perception of Krishna is constantly within our heart. And occasionally we begin to see him directly, in a way that is immediate, personal, real, and not at all a product of intellectual synthesis or projection.

As *divine love* bears fruit in the heart, these direct experiences of Krishna become uncannily detailed, well beyond the own wildest powers of imagination. Eventually we are completely transformed by a direct, uninhibited face-to-face encounter with the dark-beauty, Śyāmasundara Krishna - as described in Chapter Nine. Finally, we not only perceive the Absolute Godhead, we entered into his name, form, qualities, and pastimes to interact directly with him in an indescribable relationship of divine love.

Appendix A: Notes

Falling in (Divine) Love

I cannot get *bhakti* by changing my hairstyle, wardrobe, cosmetics, or name. I cannot get it by joining or leaving any religion or social group. I can't get it by changing where I live, or when I wake up, or what I eat. I can't get by following rules… or by breaking them. All the rituals and magic in the world will not make it materialize, nor can I grasp it by studying every book, every commentary, and every philosophy there is to study. Nothing I give away can give *bhakti* to me. Nothing can bring me any closer nor push me any further from *bhakti*. No luck, chance, fate, fortune, or other blind mercy will bring *bhakti* into my heart.

Then how? How can I get *bhakti*?

It is beautifully simple: *Only love can create love*. I cannot get divine love until I encounter someone who has it. It is like a virus, and we have to try to become infected by someone who is already infected.

How?

The air within the divine lover moves past the *bhakti*-saturated core of their heart as it travels upwards, past their vocal chords, through their lips, and emerges in the sensorial world as a pronunciation of the beloved's name, "Krishna", "Govinda", "Śyāmasundara" - a proclamation of the beloved's beauty, excellence, and uncommonly attractive activities. These *bhakti*-infected vibrations enter through my ears into my nervous system and thus come into contact with my own conscious core. The circuit is then complete. The transmission of the divine germ of has passed from one heart to another.

There *is no other way* to attain and nurture the seed of divine love besides opening our ears and heart ever wider to the transmissions of loving sound emanating from the hearts of divine lovers of Godhead.

Identifying Your Progress

Naturally we want to know, "Where am I in terms of the nine stages of *bhakti*?"

It is more than a vanity. We measure our progress because we want to *make* progress. With regular, honest introspection we must evaluate our position and determine, "Have I moved forward over time, slid backwards, or remained stagnant?"

It's not always easy to measure our progress, because:

1. The progress of *bhakti-yoga* is like the sunrise. We start seeing the effects of dawn long before the actual sunrise. Similarly we *start* seeing *slight* effects of later stages long before we've become firmly situated in those stages.

2. Each stage of *bhakti-yoga* is *built upon* the stage below it. So, the positive symptoms of the early stages of *bhakti-yoga* will continue to exist, and even strengthen, as you attain the later stages.[1]

---

[1] A special note should be made regarding the third through fifth stages: *practice, purification,* and *fixedness.* In a sense

Let's say Devī Dāsī wants to understand her current level of progress in *bhakti-yoga.* As she introspects, she honestly finds that every now and then she experiences some slight symptoms of *taste* for devotional practices (the sixth stage). More often, but still rather infrequently, she has smaller breakthroughs where she is able to be *fixed* in her devotional practice (the fifth stage). But most of the time, she has to deal with the effort to *purify* herself through diligent *practice* (the third and fourth stages). And she finds success in this effort depending on the strength of her convictions and her opportunities to associate with advanced devotees (the first and second stages).

She can see everything from the first to the sixth stage within her self. So what stage is she in? Most likely, she is in the third stage, *practice,* because that's the level she operates on *most of the time.*

---

these are three aspects of a single stage. As soon as you begin *practice*, *purification* also begins, and the more *purification* advances the more you become *fixed* in your practice. So, the end of the third stage *(practice)* overlaps the beginning of the fifth *(fixedness)*, and the fourth *(purification)* spans them both.

Making Advancement

It is simply a mistake to think that you cannot advance to Step B until you have perfectly completed Step A. In *bhakti* everything is spiritual and eternal; nothing is ever completed in an eternal process. You'll never "complete" Step A. More importantly, a significant way to make progress in Stage A is to strive and hope for Stage B!

So *start* striving for the next stage as soon as you have gotten your bearings straight in your current stage. Striving for the higher levels goes hand-in-hand with constantly *reinforcing* the lower levels you have already attained. So never think the basics are beneath you, and never think the purer levels of *bhakti* are completely beyond your grasp.

Varieties of Conviction

Conviction (śraddhā) is "confidence that the very best thing I can possibly do is to please Krishna with my love."[1]

There are different varieties of *conviction*, graded as "higher" or "lower" on the basis of their degree of endurance and profundity.

Public conviction is something imposed upon us by social norms and pressures. If all of our family and friends are celebrating *kṛṣṇa-janmāṣṭhamī,* for example, a conviction to do the same will be forced upon us from the public. This is the lowest grade of *conviction*, because it is a relatively shallow experience and it only endures as long as the external pressure endures.

Personal conviction is far superior. It is of two types: emotional and intellectual. Further, there are two subtypes of emotional conviction: mundane and spiritual.

Mundane emotional conviction is the lowest grade of personal conviction. It results from a coincidence between one's own egoistic emotions and the stimuli of divine love. For example, a

---

[1] Viz. *Caitanya Caritāmṛta* M.22.62

mother may miss the days of caring for her young children, and therefore feel some inspiration to love the darling Son of Yaśodā. Another example: a man may want to be respected, and the society of devotees may afford him that opportunity

Intellectual conviction is based on clear, rational understanding of reality, resulting in the realization that everything except divine love is illusory, unsatisfying, and unworthy of aspiration. Persons with such conviction can quickly advance to become *fixed* in their devotional practice *(niṣṭhā)*, whereas the convictions previously discussed are barely strong enough to carry a person much past the threshold of *practice (bhajana-kriyā)*.

Spiritual-emotional conviction is the highest grade, and quickly carries a practitioner even to the stage of *addiction (āsakti)*. This is simple: selfless inclination to love and please the divine without ulterior motive. Because it is founded upon intellectual conviction,[1] all aspirants to divine love should try to adopt a more serious and intellectual demeanor as far as their inherent nature will admit.

---

[1] Viz. *Bhagavad Gītā* 18.54

What is an "Offense"?

The Sanskrit term commonly equated with *offense* is *aparādhā.* This root word in this term is *rādhā*, which means "affection." The prefix is *apa-* which means "anti-" So the word *aparādhā* literally means "anti-affection."

The English term, "offense," has the following relevant definitions in a generic dictionary:

1. *A crime against accepted standards*

2. *An endeavor to conquer or dominate*

3. *Causing displeasure*

Standards and laws exist to facilitate a peaceful society conducive to affection and receptive to the happiness it creates. Thus, to transgress such laws is a type of *anti-affection.* Devotees are given lists of rules and standards that must not be transgressed. "Don't go in the temple with your shoes on," for example. "Don't go for *darśan* wearing red or blue." We approach such lists as if they were essential things carved in spiritual stone. This is not very effective in ridding our hearts of *anti-affection*. It is much more effective to understand how each rule, principle, standard, and law is meant to facilitate the expression of affection. Then one can clearly understand how follow the law not just in its letter, but in its principle. This approach to avoiding offense is very effective and propels *anartha-nivṛtti* more swiftly than we commonly see among the masses of practitioners.

Relatively speaking, it is not so important to memorize lists of offenses to be avoided. It *is* important to realize that you should aspire to nurture *affection ("rādhā")* in your every thought, word, and interaction with the forms of Krishna readily available to you (the deity, name, etc.).

What is an "*Anartha*"?

Anartha is the term for things that block the flow of divine love.

You can get rid of ***karmic anartha*** (the desire to obtain enjoyment and avoid suffering) by practicing with more depth and seriousness. This will give you access to "higher *taste*", which quickly eliminates *karmic anartha.*

Before disappearing, those selfish desires will hide in the costume of *bhakti* and become another category of *anartha*: **exploiting *bhakti* for sense gratification**. Instead of wanting to be the boss of a successful corporation, for example, we want to be the leader of a powerful religious institution. Instead of wanting a nice house in Beverly Hills, we want a nice suite in a temple. Instead of wanting to be sexually attractive, we want to attract disciples and followers. As disturbing as this behavior certainly is, it will go away with a little serious devotional practice. Once again, to really and truly cure this *anartha*, I have to strive to enjoy the pleasure of divine love. Tasting joy in hearing about Krishna is the medicine that destroys all interest in obtaining selfish gratifications from Krishna-related activities and objects.

The worst category of *anartha* is *aparādhā,* "anti-affection." It is the most difficult stain to remove, because it is the very essence of ignorance, the diametric opposite of divine love. The only cure for anti-affection is affection.

It is well known that of all *aparādhā* the most malignant is anti-affection for practitioners of devotion. Be very mindful to affectionately counter and replace your *anti-affectionate* thoughts, feelings, words, and deeds towards such persons. If you do so diligently, all impediments to your swift and deep progress in divine love will dissolve very quickly.

If I Don't Criticize You, Who Will?

"If I don't criticize this person, who will correct him?"

The problem is that people only accept corrections from someone whose opinion they *value* and respect. Are you such a person to the person you feel the need to criticize? Probably not, to be honest. Criticism from you, then, will be futile. So you should keep quiet, period.

If you cannot tolerate silence, explain your complaint carefully to someone actually in a position to correct the person - someone the person *does* look up to and respect.

If this still proves ineffective, you have to accept that certain things are beyond your control. Put some distance between yourself and the person you feel needs correction. Then you can probably relax a bit, and concentrate more on *nāma-kīrtana,* which is exactly what you need to do to resolve and dissolve your unloving feelings towards people who are, in some ways at least, saints.

It's an Offense to Feel Offended?

"If people get so easily offended, isn't that *their* problem?"

It is not a fault for a saint to become angry when the object of their affection is criticized. In fact it would be an offense not to become angry in such situations.[1]

Even if they are at fault for being offended by you, why is that important to *you*? Your own spiritual life is at stake. *That* should be what you consider important. You have to make sure that *you* get free from the blockage of *anti-affection* towards those who have attracted some measure of attention for Krishna. Offense is subjective, not objective. It's about how people *feel*. If someone feels offended by you, you *did* offend them. Period.

---

[1] This is the 11th *anga* of *sadhana bhakti*, see BRS 1.2.111. See also *Brihat Bhagavatamrta* 1.6.102 describing Rohini becoming angry and chastizing Padmavati in Dvaraka when Padmavati tried to criticize the Vraja Vasis.

Nāma-Saṁkīrtan

Nāma means "name" - Krishna's name. *Saṁkīrtan* means "fully celebrating." In this word, *kīrtan* means celebration and the prefix *saṁ-* means fully.

If we see *saṁ-* as a prefix form of *samyak,* "fully" means utilizing all paraphernalia in the celebration of the name. *All paraphernalia* can refer to musical accompaniment, dance, etc. It can also refer to using all of one's own faculties - *senses, mind, emotions, etc.* Thus *nāma-saṁkīrtan* does not necessarily always have to be musical.

Yet another implication of *fully* comes out when we understand the prefix *saṁ-* as a prefix form of *saṅga.* Then *fully* means *en masse.*

En masse can mean with many other people, or it can mean with many other practices. *Nāma-saṁkīrtan* is the supreme emperor of all practices of devotion, and all other practices surround it like attendants.

Śrī Jīva Goswāmī explains that *nāma-saṁkīrtan* is the most powerful among the five most powerful practices of devotion:

1. Caring for the feet of Krishna's beautiful form with great affection

2. Relishing the meanings of the beautiful *Bhāgavatam*

3. Becoming close with those who have affection for beautiful Krishna, and who are naturally affectionate and of similar mood

4. Fully celebrating Krishna's name

5. Situating yourself within the borders of Mathurā

These are the principle practices that should surround and support our practice of *nāma-saṁkīrtan.*

The process of attaining divine love appears long and difficult only in so far as we ignore or downplay the central, absolute importance of *nāma-saṁkīrtan.*

Nāma-Saṁkīrtan *is* Pure Devotional Service

The most important thing I've learned about the practice of divine love is that nothing is more practical, perfect, and complete than the simple act of chanting Krishna's name. In and of itself, *nāma-saṁkīrtan* is everything that pure devotional service must be.

In *Bhakti-rasāmṛta-sindhu* (1.1.11), Śrī Rūpa defines pure devotional service as: "Expressing the endeavor to please Krishna, without diversion and without ulterior motive."

Now think about what it means to chant "Hare Krishna", especially chanting *japa* in private. You have to stop doing all sorts of other things - you have to halt your fixations on all other desires and feelings, and just sit still for a while: "without diversion."

All of this just to celebrate the name of the person you love! This is a deed that no one notices, no one pays you for, it has no fringe benefits: it is "without ulterior motive."

Celebrating the beloved name of Krishna *is* pure devotional service in the most practical, immediate, and tangibly accessible form.

Appendix B: Terminology

The great souls have cultured *bhakti-yoga* with scientifically systematic diligence. The terminology of *bhakti-yoga* therefore consists of carefully chosen Sanskrit terms conveying volumes of information through their connotations and denotations. If we become knowledgeable of these terms, we can better comprehend the path of *bhakti* in deep detail - facilitating a swifter, surer progress to the ultimate goal of divine love.

Here, I will list and briefly explain the Sanskrit terms for the most important concepts encountered in this book.

Bhakti	*Devotion / Love* A tangible expression of the intention to please someone.
Uttama bhakti	*Topmost Devotion / Divine Love* A tangible expression of the intention to please Krishna,

undiluted by other expressions, and untainted by ulterior motives.

Literally, *bhakti* means "a portion belonging to a whole." *Bhakti* is one person subsuming his being into another person. An individual ego will always strive to fulfill its desires. But when the ego is merged in the beloved it strives to fulfill the beloved's desires. We are saturated with divine love when we give our heart completely to Krishna: "I am yours. Separate from you, I do not exist at all!"

Two Categories of *Bhakti*

Sādhana	*Practice* *Sā-* means "bestowing." *-Dhana* means "wealth," something valuable. The method of attaining the valued objective is *sādhana.*
Sādhya	*Perfection* This word refers to the thing that is brought into being by practice: the goal, the objective.

The last two of the nine stages of *bhakti* are counted within the category of perfection, *sādhya.*

The previous seven - or perhaps, strictly speaking, the third through seventh stages - are counted within the category of practice, *sādhana.*

Two Subcategories of Practice

Vaidhi-Sādhana *Virtuous practice*

Vidhi means "law" - behavior that is morally right and virtuous. *Vaidhi-sādhana* is practice of devotion inspired by the desire to adhere to the highest understanding of law and virtue.

Rāgānugā-Sādhana

Emotional practice

Rāga means, "blushing with passion." *Anuga* means "following." *Rāgānugā* therefore means, "following those who blush with passion." *Rāgānugā-sādhana* is practice of devotion inspired by the desire to become like those who adore Krishna with extreme passion.

The Nine Stages of *Bhakti*

Śraddhā

Conviction
Śrad- means “heart.” *-Dhā* means “put.” *Śraddhā* means, “where you put your heart.” It refers to things we trust, believe, have faith in, and value.

Sādhu-saṅga

Saintly Association
Sādhu literally means “excellent, honest, correct, and true.” Applied to a person it denotes a “saint,” a most excellent person who is honest and correct due to being deeply in touch with the truth. *Saṅga* means to be *connected* - like limbs *(aṅga)* of a body. *Sādhu-saṅga* therefore means becoming inseparable from excellent people.

Bhajana-kriyā

Devotional Practice
Kriyā means an activity regularly and systematically performed, “practice.” *Bhajana* shares the same root as *bhakti.* Literally it means “the act of sharing.” Here sharing means sharing the *self*, uniting the hearts together. So

bhajana means "the act of uniting hearts."

Anartha-nivṛtti *Purification*

Vṛtti means "earning." *Nivṛtti* means the opposite: giving away, giving up. *Artha* means "worthy thing." *Anartha* means the opposite: unworthy things. So, *anartha-nivṛtti* means giving up unworthy things.

Niṣṭhā *Fixedness*

Sthā means to remain steadily in one place. *Niṣṭhā* means to be especially fixed, unwavering, and dedicated (to *bhajana-kriyā*).

Ruci *Taste*

Ruci means "luster." When something is lustrous it is beautiful. Beautiful things are naturally *attractive*, and easy to have a *taste* for.

Āsakti *Addiction*

Āsakti means "fastening, hooking, attaching, winding and intertwining." It indicates getting "hooked on" or "addicted to" Krishna.

Bhāva — *Awakening*
Bhava means "existence," referring especially to the spiritual substance of existence, commonly known as the "soul." *Bhāva* means something that comes from the heart, from the soul.

Prema — *Divine love*
linguistically, *prema* is a rather simple term for "love." *Pre* means "inclination towards" and *ma(n)* means "appreciation."

Six Substages of *Bhajana-Kriyā*

Utsāha-mayī — *Initial Enthusiasm*
Saha means stimulant. *Sāha* means stimulated. *Ut-* means very. *Utsāha* thus means very stimulated or enthusiastic. *Mayī* means composed of.

Ghana-taralā *Mood Swings*
Ghana means solid, steady. *Tarala* means liquid, unsteady.

Vyūḍha-vikalpā *Indecision*
Vyūḍha means expanded, multiplied. *Vikalpa* means options and the resulting uncertainty and indecision.

Viṣaya-saṅgarā *Struggle with Sense Gratification*
Viṣaya means sense-objects. *Saṅga* means inseparable connection.

Niyamākṣamā *Struggle with Devotional Practices*
Niyama means obligations. *Kṣama* means to forebear and undergo. The long "ā" formed at the junction of the two words indicates the rather unsuccessful effort to undergo devotional obligations.

Taraṅga-raṅgiṇī
Exploitation of Devotion
Taraṅga means wave, flow, or tide. *Raṅga* means to enjoy and entertain oneself. *Taraṅga-raṅginī*

therefore refers to one who "rides the tide" of initial, very preliminary success in *bhakti-yoga* for the sake of personal enjoyment.

Five Impediments to Fixedness

Laya	*Drowsiness* This word indicates sleepiness and cowardice. One lacks the motivation to pay attention.
Vikṣepa	*Distraction* This word means letting-lose, scattering. One does not control and focus one's mind.
Apratipatti	*Disinterest* *Pratipatti* means to definitely and clearly perceive something. The prefix "a-" creates the opposite meaning. Despite paying attention, we lack the ability to clearly perceive anything spiritual in our practices. The root and effect of this is stubborn disinterest.

Kaṣāya *Deep Desires*
The word literally means a dye, and specifically refers to a stain upon the heart.

Rasāsvāda *(No) Enjoyment*
Rasa means deliciousness. *Svāda* means to taste. The prefix "a-" formed at the juncture of the two words introduces a double-meaning: Too much taste for the deliciousness of mundane gratifications, not enough taste for the deliciousness of divine love.

Two Degrees of Taste

Apekṣiṇī-ruci *Dependent Taste*
Apekṣā means dependence. This type of taste is conditional, dependent on circumstances. One can gain a taste for devotional practices, but only when the conditions are just right.

Anapekṣinī-ruci *Independent Taste*
The prefix "*An-*" negates the

meaning of *apekṣa,* creating the meaning, "independent."

Five Flavors of Affection

Two terms are common to all the nomenclature of the five flavors of affection: *rati* and *rāsa.* ***Rati*** means loving attraction. ***Rāsa*** means enjoying the deliciousness of *rati.*

Śānta-rāsa *Appreciation*
Śanti means peace. The disturbances of divorced-ego, and the selfish desires arising there from, have ended. In the resulting peace, one begins to truly appreciate the divine.

Dāsya-rāsa *Usefulness / Servitude*
Dāsa means lowliness and servitude. In addition to the former appreciation for the divine, one develops an active ***prīti*** (affection) that makes one desire to be useful to the divine, despite the persistent awareness of one's own infinitesimal lowliness and insignificance.

Sakhya-rāsa *Camaraderie / Friendship*
A *sakha* is a "pal." The awareness of one's lowliness is erased by the power of one's loving desire to be useful to the divine, and one steps forward to play equal, friendly roles to please Krishna as a peer.

Vātsalya-rāsa *Guardianship / Parenthood*
A *vatsa* is a calf, the symbol of a child. One's affection for the divine is so overwhelming that one perceives Krishna to be in *need* of one's protection and guidance. One therefore adopts the role of a parent or guardian of the divine.

*Ujjvala-**rāsa*** *Romance*
Indirect terms are used as names of this phenomenon. *Ujjvala* literally means "brilliant." Another term sometimes used in place of *ujjvala* is *mādhurya*, "honey-sweet." When a sense of ***priyatā*** (beloved-ness) arises, one's divine love can escalate to the most intimate level, in which

one becomes involved in the
divine romance of Krishna.

Two Forks of Spiritual Development

The two categories of practice lead to two categories of perfection.

Vaidhi-sādhana leads to "*vaidhi-bhakty-uttha*" perfection (which literally, simply means "perfection that arises from *vaidhi-sādhana-bhakti.*"). *Rāgānugā-sādhana* leads to *"rāga-bhakty-uttha"* perfection.

The perfection of divine love arising from *vaidhi-sādhana* is lesser than that arising from *rāgānugā-sādhana* simply because the nature of the former is a sense of obligation, while the nature of the later is pure loving joy.

The lesser perfection from *vaidhi-sādhana* is not intense enough to grant the three highest forms of divine intimacy: friendship, parenthood, and romance. Thus this perfection does not grant direct access to Krishna in Vṛṇdāvana. It therefore is the urgent requirement of all who aspire for divine love *of Krishna* to situate themselves within devotional practices inspired by the desire to become like the passionate associates of Krishna in Vṛṇdāvana *(rāgānugā-sādhana).*

Appendix C:
Why Our Japa Still Stinks

We pick up our *japa-mālā*... and feel disappointed. Yet again, another few hours spent without much tangible gain. Yet again, another day where all we can really say is, "Well Krishna, at least I didn't totally give up... yet."

We walk into *nāma-saṁkīrtan*... and walk out later. The best we seem to muster is the attentiveness to scrutinize the musical content or some other external detail. In consolation for our lameness, we can only say, "Well, Krishna, at least I was there... for a while."

This is not really what we gave up a normal life for. This is not the bliss and self-realization we were promised and we gambled everything on. We want attentive, powerful, soul-transforming *nāma-japa*! We were promised enthusiastic, emotionally moving, heart-rousing *kīrtan*!

From time to time we wake up enough to want to do something about it, but our efforts are usually a flurry of flailing in the dark. Thus our enthusiasm for "*japa* reform" exhausts itself pretty quick, with very little gained. We shuffle dutifully back to tolerating the taste of stale bread when the menu calls for nectar.

Why are our efforts so futile? Is this impossible? Was Mahāprabhu just a madman, and people like Śrīla Prabhupāda just propagators of a fantastic hoax?

No. Krishna is reality, and he is unmitigated bliss. It is our efforts that are remiss.

What's wrong with our efforts?

If you try to build the seventh floor without first building the other six, should you expect the structure to stand? That's what most of our reform efforts are like! We try to improve our attentiveness, but attentiveness is the *seventh step* of the process. Instead of jumping to the seventh floor, if we proceed there through the first six, we will get somewhere. If we make even a minimal effort to comprehend and implement the six preliminary steps, suddenly our efforts to improve our *nāma-bhajan* will start to *work*. We will start to chant attentively, powerfully, emotionally, and from the heart.

Overview of the Eight Steps

What are these steps I am talking about? They are the eight steps of meditation, outlined by Patanjali in the *Yoga Sūtra* as a *generic template* various schools tailor and elaborate upon to define their specific *sādhana*. If we understand the template a little better, we will understand the specific refinement a lot better. In other words, if we better understand the eight steps of meditation in general, we will better understand how to improve our specific type of meditation: *nāma-bhajan*.

Patanjali's template has eight steps:

1. Treating others properly *(yama)*

2. Treating yourself properly *(niyama)*

3. Physical preparations *(āsana)*

4. Calming down *(prāṇāyāma)*

5. Letting go *(pratyāhāra)*
6. Holding on *(dhāraṇā)*
7. Concentrating *(dhyāna)*
8. Going deeper *(samādhi)*

The first step enables the second, and so on. That's why they are sequentially enumerated. So, the attention you pay to an earlier step pays off in the later steps. We want to at least chant attentively. That's "concentration" - the seventh step. If you work a bit on steps one through six, you will find it surprisingly *possible* to do your *nāma-bhajan* in a concentrated, attentive manner.

Yama

The first step is to control how you treat others. Basically, we have to stop exploiting others for our own aims, and instead start offering ourselves to their service. Besides generating self-control, this creates a *service mentality* - both of which are essential for implementing the later steps of meditation.

Patanjali gives five specific suggestions for controlling how you treat others.

1. **Don't be violent or harmful**. Consider too how this impacts what you eat.

2. **Be truthful.**

3. **Don't steal.**

4. **Practice sexual restraint.**

5. **Don't hoard**.

Sexual restraint is more important than we would like to admit at first, because it controls a primal way in which we attempt to utilize others for pleasure. To improve your *bhajan,* limit your sexual activity. At least limit it to the confines of a relationship in which you are seriously committed to serve the long-term good of your sexual partner. Better, limit it to the confines of procreation. Finally, when the time is right in your life, limit it entirely.

Practice these five principles and many other ways of improving how you treat other people, and everything else about your meditation will be much easier to improve.

Niyama

Now, improve how you treat yourself. Live your life in a way that eliminates causes of distraction and facilitates attentiveness to the divine. Patanjali gives five specific suggestions:

1. **Be clean.** Disorganization = distraction, the antithesis of attentive meditation.

2. **Be satisfied.** Don't always want more; desiring external things distracts the mind from *bhajan*.

3. **Minimize**. Become more spartan. This will erase zillions of distractions.

4. **Educate yourself**. Build your mental muscles. You need them to concentrate on your *bhajan*. Although any education is good, it's particularly effective to educate yourself on the science of *bhajan* and the object of your meditation: Krishna-*nāma*.

5. **Be godly**. See divinity everywhere. See people as souls, and Krishna as the soul of those souls. See objects as divine energy.

Āsana

Meditation itself starts by sitting down: *āsana.* The essential principle for how to "sit properly" is *sukhaṁ sthiraṁ āsana* - **"Sit in a way that is comfortable yet firm."**

It has to be *comfortable*, so that you don't get distracted by physical aches and pains. To that end there is some merit to doing a few daily stretches and exercises so that your body isn't in awful shape and very prone to aches and pains.

It can't be *so* comfy that it lulls you to sleep. So it needs to be *"firm", too.* How do you sit "comfortably yet firmly"? Basically, just *sit up straight.*

A few practical suggestions:

- Sit in a place that isn't distracting.
- Sit "Indian style." That means, sit on the floor with your legs folded. Ask a yoga teacher to show you "sukhāsana, siddhāsana, or padmāsana" if you're totally unsure how to fold your legs.
- Keep your back straight. You accomplish this by trying to be *tall* when you sit.

- Trying to be *tall* will also help you keep your neck straight and your head centered.
- Relax your shoulders so they *hang*, but don't let them slouch forward.

Prāṇāyāma

You're sitting comfortably and firmly, so now it's time to *calm down*. You can't concentrate on anything when you're not calm!

How do you calm down?

Breathe.

How do you breathe correctly? Essentially, just breathe *deeply* and *steadily*. It's more effective to breathe from your stomach than from your chest. Push the stomach out to pull air in. Squeeze the stomach in to push air out. With a tiny bit of practice you'll get the hang of it.

Why does this calm the mind?

Well, for one thing, oxygen seems to make the brain sharp. But, besides that, steady breathing provides a bit of a "metronome" clicking off a calm rhythm which provides a foothold on which you can more easily pull yourself up and into meditation. Keep your *mantra* going *in sync* with your breathing pattern! Between that and sitting up straight, you'll never fall asleep or get drowsy during your *nāma-bhajan* again.

One suggestion for how to chant the *mahā-mantra* in sync with your breathing: Exhale for a certain number of repetitions, I suggest three. Then, do another half at the very end of the exhalation, and inhale sharply while doing the second half of the fourth repetition. You can still pronounce this part easily while you inhale.

Pratyāhāra

When you are sitting right and have calmed down, take the next step: *let go*. Stop all your thoughts.

This tends to stop us dead in our tracks. We feel powerless to let go of all the thoughts that constantly dominate our mind. It seems impossible. After trying many different approaches with various degrees of failure, I stumbled on a technique that works: Don't try to let go of your thoughts, *let go of your identity*.

If you let go of your identity, you automatically let go of your thoughts because identity is the root of thought. The person we think we are determines the things we want, and the things we want cause the flood of incessant thoughts in our minds.

Before we can do attentive *nāma-bhajan* we have to let go of the person we think we are. We have to change our identity, and the first step is letting go of our existing sense of self.

Sitting firmly, breathing calmly, tell yourself, "I am not 'me.' I am not this body. I have *nothing* to do with anything my body is implicated in. I have no past. I have no future. I have no family. I have no friends. I have no enemies, no debts, no responsibilities. All of that is unreal. Now I have disconnected from it all."

Dhāraṇā

Dhāraṇā means to "hold the shape." We have discarded our false shape, and now we must assume of our true shape. Letting go of our false self, all the thoughts flowing from it ceased. Our mind became effortlessly silent and empty. Now we have the space in which to create a true self-image - an identity that will welcome and adore the Holy Name with a flood of affectionate and attentive thought. We have shut off the false self, based on a body. Now we must turn on the true self, based on the soul.

You must envision your true self according to your honest inspiration and capacity, but it should have as little as possible to do with the mundane self you currently project in the illusory world. Regardless of the details, the bottom line is that we must step outside of our mundane identity and assume a transcendental sense of self. To introduce some details: Envision yourself as a person fit for, but still aspiring to achieve, a specific type of intimate devotional service to the Supreme Personality, Sri Krishna. You may see yourself as a young boy aspiring to assist Krishna's friends. You may see yourself as an adult aspiring to assist Yaśodā or Nanda in raising their dear child, Krishna. You may see yourself as an exquisite young lady aspiring to assist Śrīmatī Rādhārāṇī in delighting the transcendental romantic, Krishna. However you see yourself, don't skimp on the detail. Figure it out with your heart and *get into the role*.

When you get into the role of a person whose identity is built upon Krishna, extraneous thoughts in your mind will disappear and your mental environment will become extremely hospitable towards the Holy Name.

If you insist that you're not qualified for this, you shoot yourself in the foot. There is no qualification to want to please Krishna in a particular way, other than simply having the sincere desire to please Krishna in a particular way. If somehow you cannot yet find an honest spark of inspiration for a particular type of relationship with Krishna, then assume the identity of a faceless being and make your first order of *bhajan* the expression of desire to acquire a face that Krishna can look upon and a personality he can enjoy.

Bhajan is a personal affair. Don't "tweet status updates" about the private details of your *bhajan*. If and when you must, speak of it only for the sake of helping others improve their own *bhajan*, without needlessly revealing intimate personal details. What goes on in our divine meditation is much more private than our normal concept of "private life." Avoid exhibitionism, because there is the risk of wanting to be better than others or trying to impress them, which will pollute your spiritual self-concept, forcing you to backtrack and start all over again.

If you sit up straight and breathe systematically, you won't doze off. If you let go of your false identity and assume the role of a true identity, you won't be distracted. So, by following these four steps you will be at least halfway to genuine *niṣṭhā-bhajan.*

Dhyāna

Once you are mentally "in the role", *nāma-bhajan* is relatively easy and effortless. Attentive japa and heartfelt *kīrtan* will blossom. Spiritual bliss will cease to be only a dream or a theory. All you need to do now is pronounce the name. The rest will be easy and effortless. Simply pronounce the name with your mouth, and hear it with your ear.

I have found that the louder I chant, the easier it is to let the mind wander. The mouth can keep doing the mantra while the mind does something else. Therefore, I like to gradually make my chanting quieter and quieter, eventually becoming inaudible to the external ear. As the external vibration becomes quieter, the internal vibration must become louder. The internal vibration happens "in the mind" - it is produced by the subtle tongue and heard by the subtle ear. When the mental tongue and ear are responsible for chanting and hearing, if the mind wanders at all the chanting will immediately come to a dead stop. This allows us to detect and correct distraction more rapidly and effectively.

Similarly, I have found that the slower I chant, the more my mind wanders. It takes less effort to chant at a leisurely pace. Therefore it is easier to "space out." The faster I chant, the more effort I have to make to insure that I am still forming all the syllables of the mantra correctly. The more effort I put in, the more naturally I remain focused and attentive.

So, my practical suggestion is to strive for "quick and quiet" *mantra japa*. But regardless of the specific technique, the essence of *dhyāna* is to *hear* the sound of the mantra, not just with your external ear, but with your *consciousness*.

What does it mean to "hear with your consciousness"? When you hear the sound of a word, the meaning of the word naturally awakens in your thoughts. When you hear the sound of a name, the person who is named is invoked within your thoughts. So when you hear the name Krishna, naturally the person Krishna will appear in your heart - accompanied by all his qualities and beauty, so wonderfully expressed in his sweet pastimes.

This is not an impossible dream. This is a *practice* meant for *you and I* to do *on a daily basis.* This is the powerful medicine that cures the heart and bestows divine love. As long as you think this is something not meant for you, you will never achieve it. As long as you think you are inadequate you will remain inadequate. Yes we are fallen and inadequate, but that is not our intrinsic nature. We are adequate to be empowered by *bhakti*, because we are the divine energy of Śrī Krishna! Why do you insist that you must remain inadequate!? Allow yourself to be empowered by the omnipotent Goddess of Devotion. Allow yourself to desire Krishna in a particular way, to call his name in that mood. Allow that name to manifest transcendental reality within your awareness.

Samadhi

When the divine name of Śrī Krishna manifests within your awareness - you will be forcefully drawn into "*samādhi.*" The more deeply the name pulls you into its beauty, qualities and pastimes, the more fully you enter *samādhi.*

Strive to expose yourself to *samādhi* every day in your *nāma-bhajana.* Eventually the name will pull you *all the way in* and you will disappear from the realm of illusion. This is "*samādhi*" in the final sense. You will tangibly enter the living, real, immediate company of Śrī Krishna - in the role that you desired and cultivated. And you will never re-enter the false world of selfishness.

Understanding the Words

The meanings within the divine names of the Hare Krishna *mahā-mantra* are infinitely deep. They manifest themselves very personally and intimately to each and every one of us with unique peculiarities and specifics, reflecting our own uniqueness of being and the divine's own infinitude.

The more deeply we comprehend meaning in the sound vibrations, the more vibrantly those words will manifest their non-different contents within our perception. So, we should make great efforts to understand the words of the *mantra* as deeply as possible.

Here is one description of the meaning of the names in the Hare Krishna *mahā-mantra:*

Hare

Hare means "ravishing," "captivating," and "carrying away." It is the brilliant, sparkling energy of attraction and affection that radiates from lustrously black Krishna. *Hare* refers to:

- Krishna's Devotees:
    - Śrīmatī Rādhārāṇī and the young *gopīs*
    - Yaśodā, Nanda, and so on
    - Subāla and the young *gopas*
    - Raktak and the servants of Krishna
- The *gaura-līlā* equivalents
    - Mahāprabhu and his associates
    - Gadādhara
    - Rūpa, Ragunātha, and all the ācāryas.

Krishna

Krishna means "all-attractive." He is the lustrous black-hole swallowing up the breath, hearts, attention, and desires of everyone - the gravity-well of infinite beauty, charm, wit, allure, etc.

The meaning of the word "Krishna" will reflect the meaning of the word "Hare" it is coupled with. For example, if the devotee experiences "Hare" to be Krishna's mother, Yaśodā, the "Krishna" coupled with that "Hare" will most likely be the very young boy that mother Yaśodā so adores. If on the other hand, the devotee experiences "Hare" to be Rādhārāṇī, the associated "Krishna" will reveal himself as the adolescent romantic.

Rāma

Rāma means "pleasure." He is the brilliant super-nova of pleasure, ecstasy, and bliss - an explosion of transcendent joy. "Rāma" can assume many forms, such as:

- Rādhā-rāmana - Krishna as the instrument of Śrīmatī Rādhārāṇī's pleasure.
- Nityānanda Rāma
- Balarāma

If one experiences "Hare" as Śrī Rādhā, the accompanying "Rāma" reveals himself as Rādhā-rāmana. If one experiences "Hare" as Gaurahari, the accompanying "Rāma" reveals himself as Nityānanda Rāma.

Thus there are infinite ways to understand and "translate" the *mahā-mantra*. The general overtone invoked by repeating "Hare" so many times, however imparts the meaning that we are imploring

Krishna to engage us. "Oh Krishna, take me! Make me yours!"

I hope the above explanation of the names in the divine *mantra* will fuel your own intuitively deep celebration of the name.

Appendix D: Śikṣāṣṭaka

1

ceto-darpaṇa-mārjanam

It polishes the heart's mirror.

bhava-mahā-dāvāgni-nirvāpaṇaṁ

It extinguishes the raging fire burning this worldly forest.

śreyaḥ-kairava-candrikā-vitaraṇaṁ

It is the moonlight that impels the white lotus of good fortune to blossom.

vidyā-vadhū-jīvanam

It inspires and enlivens knowledge.

ānandāmbudhi-vardhanaṁ

It swells the ocean of bliss,

prati-padaṁ pūrṇāmṛtāsvādanaṁ

And always grants the deepest taste of that nectar.

sarvātma-snapanaṁ

It is the sacred bath that fully purifies every aspect of "self."

What is it?

paraṁ vijayate śrī-kṛṣṇa-saṅkīrtanam

It is the supremely victorious congregational celebration of Śrī Krishna!

2

Krishna: How do you perform my celebration, "*Śrī Krishna Saṁkīrtan*"?

nāma-nāma

By chanting your holy name, over and over again!

What makes my name so powerful that it can bestow the blessings you just described?

akāri bahudhā nija-sarva-śaktiḥ.

You have invested all your own potencies into the sound of your many names.

Since the name is as powerful as I, it must be dangerous! Only the most qualified people should be able to utilized it, no?

tatrārpita niyamitaḥ smaraṇe na kālaḥ.

No! Anyone, anywhere, at any time can remember your holy name and use it effectively!

That is amazing! How can something so valuable and powerful be available to everyone and anyone?

etādṛśī tava kṛpā bhagavan!

Yes it is amazing! Just see how compassionate you are, All-Attractive Krishna!

Then why isn't everyone doing Krishna-nāma-saṁkīrtana all the time???

mamāpi durdaivam īdṛśam ihājani nānurāgah.

We have no natural affection for you. Just see how unfortunate we all are!

3

This is so sad. What can you do about it?

tṛṇād api sunīcena
taror iva sahiṣṇunā
amāninā mānadena
kīrtaniyaḥ sadā hariḥ

We will constantly sing your *kīrtan* -

Admitting our misfortune, and thus calling your name more humbly than grass

Tolerating the difficulty as patiently as a tree

Never thinking we deserve any admiration, and always finding something to admire in others.

4

Why should you struggle so hard to perform my *nāma-saṁkīrtan*? What is it for?

na dhanaṁ

Not for money

na janaṁ

Not for friends, family or followers

na sundarīṁ

Not to impress the opposite sex

kavitaṁ vā

Not for erudition

jagadīśa kāmaye

I desire none of the things my Universal Master could so easily bestow.

Then what *do* you ask from me?

mama janmani janmanīśvare

"My dear Master, life after life,

bhavatād bhaktir akaitukī tvayi

All I want is to have pure love for you!"

5

All you want is love? Don't you also want to come to me?

ayi nanda-tanūja

Alas, Son of Nanda!!!

kiṅkaraṁ patitaṁ māṁ viṣame bhavāmbudhau

I am your fallen servant, drowning in the ocean of worldly poison.

kṛpayā tava-pāda paṅkaja-sthita-dhūlī

Out of compassion, you might make me a particle of pollen on the lotus flower of your feet,

sadṛśaṁ vicintaya

Whenever you think I deserve it.

6

When do you think I might feel you deserve it?

nayanaṁ galad-aśru-dhārayā

When tears fall from their pools welled up in my eyes...

vadanaṁ gadgada-ruddhayā girā

When my words cannot escape the stuttering in my mouth...

pulakair nicitaṁ vapuḥ kadā

When goose bumps cover my entire body...

tava nāma-grahaṇe

...each time I embrace your name.

When will this time come!?

bhaviṣyati

...someday.

7

Make it come sooner! I have become hungry for your love!!!

yugāyitaṁ nimeṣeṇa

Each moment drags on like an age

cakṣuṣā prāvṛṣāyitam

My eyes destroy the worlds with their flooding torrents

śūnyāyitaṁ jagat sarvaṁ

Everything in the universe becomes nothing... all is void...

govinda-viraheṇa me

Because I am still without you, Govinda.

8

I am speechless and in awe of your pure love. I want to comprehend it myself. I want to taste it. Please let me know your inner heart. How do you feel when you wait in the forest grove for me in the dead of night, unsure if I will show up at all?

āśliṣya vā

Maybe he will embrace me?

pāda-ratāṁ pinaṣṭu mām

Maybe he will trample me under his feet...

adarśanān marma-hatāṁ karotu vā

Or maybe he will absolutely break my heart,

By not showing up at all.

yathā tathā vā vidadhātu

He may do this.

Or he may do that.

lampaṭo

He is, truly, a debauchee.

mat-prāṇa-nāthas tu

But I can *breathe* only for him!

sa eva nāparah

And there can never be anyone else for me!